A W

A Single Mother's Journey Through Advanced Breast Cancer

Deena Nehring

Deena Nehring

DEDICATION

For my mother, my guardian angel.

Deena Nehring

Acknowledgements

A big thank you to all my family and friends who cheered me on during this entire process; it was your collective encouragement which helped make this book possible.

To my fiancé, thank you for your continued support and encouragement, as well as for understanding and putting up with me during this entire process. You are my one and only true knight 'in slightly tarnished armor'. I love you.

To my daughter, thank you for your computer expertise with graphic design and all that other complicated computer "stuff" that always looks and sounds "Greek" to me. You rock!

Last, but not least, a HUGE thank you goes out to my friend Jonie for helping me with the entire editing process itself.

Hope...the most beautiful word I know

Authors Note...

I've always been a firm believer that everybody who passes through our lives has a purpose. No matter if that connection is for mere seconds, days, weeks, months, or even years, everybody who comes in to our life is meant to be there for a reason.

This concept of mine was validated in July of 2008. That's when I met Mike. Now Mike and I were from two totally different walks of life. Him: the recovering addict who'd beat his addiction, found God, and had made it his life work assisting others in overcoming their own addictions. Me: what he'd referred to as the "good girl", a clean-cut straight-laced single mother of three, juggling college, kids, and well basically just trying to make ends-meet. Night and day we were, but none the less, our lives collided and we'd hit it off. Oh, it was nothing serious, mind you, just your basic courtship; both of us simply enjoying each other's company and exploring where things might lead. That itself lasted a mere three weeks. Yet, that short time span was more than enough time for Mike to complete his divine task. How so, you may ask. Well, he saved me. He noticed then simply mention "the lump". In doing so, he literally saved my life. Sounds crazy, I know. But, if Mike had chosen to not say anything at all, well chances are I probably wouldn't be here today explaining any of this. Because, you see, at the time of detection that lump wasn't just a lump. It had already begun to spread.

So whatever happened to the man who literally saved my life? We took our own paths. But once in a blue moon we bump in to each other. When we do we always exchange a bear-hug and after a quick catch-up we simply stare at each other and sigh. He always comments, "Wow. Aren't you glad I mentioned it?" and I always smile, nod and then reply, "Yes. Thank you..."

I will never ever be able to even begin to thank him enough...

To succeed in life, you need three things: a wishbone, a backbone and a funnybone. —Reba McEntire

CHAPTER 1

It's always something.
—*Roseanne Roseannadanna (Gilda Radner)*

Wednesday July 23, 2008

The surgeon called today—called me, himself. It had only been a day or two since my mammogram and ultrasound, so I wasn't expecting a phone call this soon. Let alone have those results delivered by the surgeon himself. Sheer befuddlement, it seemed, would now be the theme for the remainder of the day. I remember discovering the lump. How could I forget? It was a Friday night; date night. A man that I had been seeing had noticed it—the lump that is…all due to a frisky goodnight kiss and grope. *You should really have that checked out…*he'd commented the next morning during a phone call. I promised him that I would, that I would call my doctor first thing Monday morning.

Strange…, while it usually takes pulling eyeteeth to get an appointment within the same week you called, for some reason all I had to say was lump in my armpit by my boob, and they squeezed me in that day. Of course I figured a mammogram and ultrasound would be ordered…but not stat, and not for that same afternoon. What threw me however, what really threw me, was my doctor's query of: *"Who do you prefer for a surgeon?"*

Okay so it's a lump. I was a little freaked out. But it wasn't a big deal. So why would I need a surgeon? Still under the belief that this was not—could not be—anything serious, my reply had been: *"I don't know. Pick whomever you think is best…"*. And now that 'pick whomever you think is best' was calling me himself. I guess somewhere in the depths of my mind, I knew why. But, you see, denial is a funny creature. It has an uncanny ability to cloak itself within a hodgepodge of emotions. Panic and confusion at its best, receiving a personal call from the surgeon they had picked. And denial… For the life of me, I still could not fathom why my regular OBGYN office hadn't made this routine call themselves.

After a brief introduction, Dr. Beckley began fostering our soon to be surgeon-patient bond with frankness, by saying, "Look, I hear you're a nurse, so I'll cut through the normal BS. Got your mammogram and ultrasound in front of me and I need you in my office as soon as possible."

Bam, bam, bam…just like that.

"Um….okay…?" Baffled, my hesitance probably came across as sheer annoyance.

In all truth, I was annoyed. I was distracted. I was busy. My life was already beyond hectic. I was a single mom, juggling three kids and running a household single-handed. I had just spent an exhausting three years in college. I had recently graduated and all I wanted to do was return to a semi-normal lifestyle; pass my nursing exam, start my new career, and provide for my children. I did not have time for more appointments. I was too busy cramming; preparing to sit for the NCLEX (the state nursing exam).

Ironic that, at the time, I viewed taking and passing

that very exam as my biggest life challenge…

"When?" I inquired, impatient. Half expecting to be transferred to the receptionist in order to set up the day and time, I eyed my calendar for the next possible opening that I could possibly manage to squeeze in yet another appointment.

"Right now," was his reply; apparently this was my only option.

Right now….? As in drop everything and come in right now? In all truth, I'm not even sure now if I actually blurted those thoughts out loud, or what my actual response was, other than sheer and utter panic as I listened to his instructions of by-passing the regular check in process and to come straight to his office, before ending the actual call.

Blindsided, I stood in my kitchen; phone in one hand, daily planner in the other. I helplessly stared at the mess of open books, study flash cards and note binders scattered across my kitchen table as everything blurred and my life skidded to a screeching halt. In that split second I knew, somehow had already sensed it. My bright future, those well laid plans, the nursing career I was so eager to begin…all of it had just been altered by those two simple words: *Right now…*

*   *   *

Pulling out of the garage, I broke down and called my mom. I don't know why really? I was thirty-eight years old; a grown woman; an adult. By now however I felt like a frightened child (although I wouldn't admit that then). I was scared, confused, and just needed to hear her voice, longed for the comfort that only a mother's voice could deliver.

All I really wanted was for her to reassure me that this was nothing and that everything would turn out fine. And although I knew better, I think I actually wanted her to tell me that this was normal practice: for a surgeon himself to call and request your immediate presences within his office. That any of it was no big deal.

But those words: *right now....right now....right now!!!!* had already snagged on a continuous loop within my mind. And I couldn't erase the deafening roar of those two words from my head. So I needed my mother to tell me this wasn't a big deal; that I was making mountains out of molehills. Yet, while I explained the brief conversation that I had just had—once I disclosed to her that it had been Dr. Beckley who had called me himself—I detected the trepidation clouding her rapid-fire questions. Heard the tearful hiccup of disquiet unease when she announced, "I'm already on my way."

I'm not really sure how long I sat there. On autopilot, I didn't even recall the short drive let alone pulling into a space within the parking lot of Medical Associates itself, with my cell phone still pressed to my ear. It didn't matter, really as my mother was pulling into the busy parking lot herself. Embarrassment washed over me once I realized it. Scolding myself, I flipped my cell phone shut then forced myself to get out of my car. I hadn't needed my mother to accompany me to a doctor's appointment since...well, since I was little girl. Yet, for some reason, seeing her, having her there, however embarrassing it may have seemed it also somewhat calmed my nerves. I was relieved. I wanted—no, I needed her to be there with me.

After a brief run through of the same exact conversation we'd just had via cell phones, we then really didn't speak much. I guess because we were both nervous. Although neither of us would dare acknowledge that fact out loud to the other. I detected fear within her eyes when she asked again, "Doctor Beckley, himself, called?" Nodding in conformation, I myself did not want to talk about it....the reasons, the possibilities, the whys. I was still annoyed, a tad bit reluctant to even be there. My mother was uncharacteristically edgy. But I didn't have the guts to ask her why. As instructed I skipped the otherwise normal process of standing in line and checking in with the main reception and we went straight downstairs to Dr. Beckley's office, stopping at his receptionist.

As we sat, before we could even get ourselves settled, Dr. Beckley himself strolled out in to the waiting area, full of purpose. He stopped mid stride upon seeing my mother; his entire face lit up with surprised delight and his cheerful salutation boomed above the office scuttlebutt. I have to admit, it broke the tension simmering just below the knot of uneasy trepidation clutching my gut. I was relieved as I now remembered this certain surgeon instantly.

He had the type of presents a person just did not forget. He was professional, with an animated yet laidback disposition. He was straight-up cool. And if I had to choose only a single word to describe this man as a doctor, it would have to be: unpretentious. I remembered that, him, from during my clinical rotation on the surgical floor.

I waited and watched the exchange of warm greetings between he and my mother, which ended with Dr. Beckley quizzing her to why she was even there in the first place. She gave him a lopsided frown while pointing toward me and half laughed, "This is Deena. My daughter. The one you needed to see right now...?"

As his friendly yet puzzled gaze locked on mine, I acknowledged him with a 'yep-that's-me-here-I-am' half smile, then sat quietly staring back at this man; watching his once jovial expression distorted to that of what looked to be a mix of fear and staggered shock.

"No—? Really?" he exclaim, befuddlement now threatening his cheerful tone he pursued with, "She yours?" Pausing yet again, his gazed bounced between us and he managed to recover that more jovial air. "Get out! She belongs to you—?"

"Afraid so," my mother laughed, then announced proudly, "This is the daughter I told you about. The one who just graduated from the nursing program."

"Yes. Yes. Now I remember." Glancing between us yet again, the disbelief within his voice fluctuated to something I couldn't quite pin down. And as I sat there listening to their rather amusing bout of idle chit-chat between them, I noted the poignant expression he wore once his gaze found mine. He then just stood there staring at me, the unease creeping back in. "So...she belongs to you," he sighed and as if trying to dispute the very fact that I was indeed his former patient's child.

His attention toggled back to my mother as he mentioned something about surnames and not having had put it together at first. We all chuckled at that of course, but our chorus of laughter barely dented the newest layer of tension.

Yes, I was her daughter. The person this man had just spoken to himself via the phone. The soon to be patient who he'd requested to see in his office *right now*...and for reasons still unknown. The daughter of a former patient of his. You see, my own mother had recently—again, been battling cancer herself on and off for the past couple of years. And this man, this wonderful and talented doctor, had been her surgeon at one time.

Turning to the very reason why I was there, he ushered us into an exam room and his focus was now on me and the results of my mammogram and ultrasound. Because I was a recent nursing graduate, he told me again that he was sparing me the normal BS as he explained the reasons of why he had asked me to come in. I can't remember the entire conversation, and despite the subject matter, the beat was light and carefree as if nobody had a concern in the world. Dr. Beckley is good that way. He has a wonderful bedside manner. Like I said, he is straight-up cool. As we spoke of all the possibilities, what stuck in my mind was his announcement that I was just too young for all of this. That it was uncommon for women of my age to get breast cancer. Okay, I know this....great. So why do you keep repeating this fact? Better yet, why am I now here sitting in your office?

As if reading my mind, he went on to further explain to

me that if (or when) women my age did get breast cancer, it was usually the deadliest type; an extremely rapid growing and very aggressive form, of which, typically presented itself as a lump under the armpit. The unspoken part: hence, the very reason I was now there sitting in his office. More confusion settled within me...because I could sense it; could see it written all over his face. That unspoken part. And I just couldn't believe that this doctor had simply requested my presence within his office to tell me I was too young...reassure me that it probably wasn't cancer. I don't think he realized that he was scaring the hell out of me with stories of others my age or younger who had already been effected...who had died. And let's not forget the unspoken: the odd chance that this might actual be cancer because of its location... But for some reason he just wouldn't outright say that part of the equation. We just keep circling around the issue itself.

As he continued to dance around the topic, I nodded accordingly, mind racing yet now locked in fear and unable to keep track of the discussion. The possibilities, the probabilities, the odds, the whys, the hows—his very words—none of it was registering within my brain. Only one fact stuck. The one which had jammed my ability to think straight: ...usually the deadliest kind, of which, typically presented itself as a lump under the armpit.

He must have sensed he'd basically lost me—I don't know, maybe I wasn't nodding accordingly anymore?—because he stopped short and motioned me to follow him to an otherwise restricted area in order to view the results myself. Although I appreciated this, I still didn't comprehend why. Sure I was a recent graduate, soon to be a licensed nurse; he was the doctor and a doctor who liked to demonstrate rather than use just words...so in effect he was teaching me. But I really could not grasp the significance of what it was he teaching, was now try to tell me, more over what it was he was trying to show me. The medical part I got...and I understood the films were mine.

It just did not register that he was referring to my very results as he explained to me the differences between the shape, size, and density of tumors and how they all grew.

He then further explained to me how they could somewhat detect whether or not a tumor was cancerous just by how it appeared on the film....all of this, of course, while still pointing to the tumors—my very own sinister looking lumps—captured within the films *(yes, I said tumors. As in plural. There were two masses adjoined and growing together that were maybe a little bit larger than the size of a small tennis ball).* I again just stood there and simply nodded and listened, as if I were again a nursing student and as if I was looking at somebody else's results.

Although I did understand his tutorial of the variety of tumors and such, on the medical aspect, I still could not understand what he was actually trying to convey. Again, the significance of why he was telling me all of this had escaped my logic. Something in my mind would not allow me to comprehend the fact that he was doing all of this, in order to somehow soften the blow, as he pointed out the sinister nature of my very own tumors on those films.

I was in denial; full blown denial. After all, I was healthy. Young; only thirty-eight years of age. I was on top of the world. Ready to get on with my life in general. Start my new career as a nurse. So despite staring at those films, seeing the ominous way those tumors presented themselves, the actual chance that they were malignant—in my mind—was remote. It just wasn't going to be so...or so I told myself.

In all actuality he already knew himself the chances of them being malignant were high. Yet, you see, he could not tell me this for fact. He could only speculate. So we had just spent the past half hour or so dancing around the subject, because he needed to do more tests. One test in particular, to substantiate or disprove the preliminary findings displayed on my very own films.

As we went back inside the small confines of the exam

room, that is when he explained he needed to do a core biopsy. And he wanted to do this procedure right now.

Mind swimming, again it was the urgency of his request which cued me to the seriousness of the situation at hand. A situation that I was unwillingly being forced to now deal with. A core biopsy....well, it just sounded so harsh and likely would be...well, painful. Don't get me wrong, I'm not a wuss. I just was not prepared to be poked, probed and or prodded by some huge gage needle.

"Right now?" I quizzed.

"Yes. We can do it right here in the office," he replied.

Ambivalent, I glance at my mom with a desperate help-me-out-here look. Some help. She gave me her 'what-do-you-want-me-to-do?' tight smile. Great... "Fine. Let's do it," I sighed. *Take a damn sample already....get it over with and let's be done with this!*

After all, it was just another test....right? A simple procedure. One of which, I was told, would take about a week before we would hear the results. He'd also informed me of the risks, and of the chance that these test results still might lead to the necessity of yet another procedure called a lumpectomy. A minor surgery. One, of which, I had agreed to during our dance around the issue conversation. It would be done in order to remove the tumors, once all their test were completed. We had already discussed that aspect—had weighed the options. Removing these unwanted tumors themselves, regardless of whether or not they were malignant, was the plan....just because he *"did not like the looks of them"*. So in my mind, this test would simply rule out that shadow of doubt which now clung within my heart.

I already knew, of course, what the results would be. I think we all did. Despite his reassurance that I was just too young for these ominous looking tumors to be growing within me, it was something within Dr. Beckley's eyes that had tipped me off early on. Something I couldn't exactly pin-point or give a name. Something of which had conflicted with his encouraging words and assuring smile throughout the course of our entire conversation. But like I said, denial is a funny creature; with an uncanny ability to mask itself. So even though I was frightened, I chose to believe that none of this was actually happening. None of it was real...therefore, there was not a chance in hell these tumors of mine were going to be malignant. I was a busy mom, ready to start my new career as a nurse. Therefore, I simply was not going to have breast cancer. I couldn't because...well, just because. I just did not have time to deal with something of such magnitude.

Journal Entry, Friday July 25th 2008

It is yet another sleepless night... I wait. I pace, and then find myself wishing I had a significant other. Not that I need one...because I don't. I'd determined this a while ago. As I'd proven I could take care of myself. But...in these types of situations, or rather these type of life moments...I have to wonder and think it'd be nice. You know, to have somebody strong hold you, kiss your forehead and tell you that everything was going to be alright. Or at least that's how I pictured it in my head. I've never had a man do or say that. I'm strictly going off what I've learned as a child from those stupid Disney fairy tales. Do men actually do that? My dad would, that's for certain. But other men my own age....um, to be honest I simply have no clue.

It doesn't matter, because I do not have a significant other (aka: a man). Don't get me wrong, I did have; a few times. And right after that third divorce, eh...I decided...well, I don't know. I just...well, let's just say I strategically keep them away; them being the male species.

Lord...maybe my mother is right. Maybe I'm just too damn stubborn and independent for my own good...?

Regardless, here I am again. It's the middle of the night and I'm sitting in front of my computer rambling....apparently typing everything that pops into my mind. I love to write...and I usually weave tales of criminal thrillers peppered with romantic suspense. Tonight however I jot down thoughts as they cartwheel through my mind and then stare blankly at the blinking curser...

It's past 2AM.. I eyeball the clock. Correction, I stare it down; as if I can somehow mentally will the time to pass faster. Ironic...instead maybe I should be trying to mentally will time to stop all together? Perhaps that would be best, stopping time all together, because I really do not want to know the results of this test...core biopsy...the recollection makes me shutter.

I fear the worst. I won't admit it aloud, but I'm honestly scared to death...

CHAPTER 2

Author's note...

Anybody who knows me, and I mean really knows me, knows that I am NOT a morning person. Furthermore, those who know me are also aware of the fact that I am not fully awake, nor fully functional, until I've had at least one cup of coffee to kick start my brain. While a patient of his, my mother apparently shared my life story with Dr. Beckley. She, however, forget to mention the above...that essential tidbit of me not being a morning person...

Friday July 25th, 2008

Sometime before 8:00AM my blissful state of slumber was rudely interrupted. Groping for, locating, and then somehow managing to flip my cell phone correctly—without peeling open my eyelids—my groggy "Hello?" was acknowledged with: "Deena...Akin Beckley. Got your biopsy results. We need to do more surgery."

Bam, bam, bam...just like that.

Now, mind you, I was still more than half asleep and struggling to just place the name. Who? To my knowledge, I did not know of any Akins. Who on earth was this person? Although the Beckley part was vaguely familiar, the Akin threw me. And without my morning dose of coffee my brain would not allow me to make the connection.

And besides it had only been a day, maybe two...? I hadn't expected to get results back this soon, let alone so ungodly early in the morning. And wow...no 'good morning' or 'hi how are you'....how about that, huh—? This person was way too curt; oddly somber and all business.

While still trying to place the name Akin, the key words: biopsy, results, surgery and we tumbled throughout my subconscious but not necessarily in that order causing a jumbled mess. Who the hell was *we*? Because according to this brutally sober voice that *we* needed more surgery! My God, none of what this man was saying made any sense. Therefore, I had to be still dreaming—correction, Mr. Sandman had apparently taken a wrong turn at the junction of blissful fantasy and strange-dream realm, and was right now barreling down the dimly lit back alley of unimaginable circumstance.

Next stop: hellish nightmare-land. All aboard! Crap— Wait—Stop! I'm on the wrong bus. Please, I need to get back on the one going to blissful dreamland...

"....just went over the results with him and we both feel..."

Still only picking up random tidbits, for some reason I at least correctly assumed this unnamed 'him' was in reference to a pathologist. Why not? It was only a nightmare, right? But who was *we*? Mind stumbling over a tangle questions as well as medical jargon (words of which I told myself I indeed knew....um, from somewhere—?), I gave up trying to decipher any of it and just went along for the ride; as the voice still trickling into my eardrum jammed even more information into my nonfunctioning brain. As the narrator of this nightmare pressed onward, it was the convincing tone of concern that set off alarms in my head and pierced my brain. This man's almost too rushed approach to tell me everything he could pertaining to those results and this *we* needing surgery—in the least amount of time, cued my lethargic body to jerk upright.

This *we* person who needed more surgery was *me*! And that meant that this Akin somebody had to be Akin Beckley...as in Doctor Akin Beckley. *Shit, shit....SHIT!* Jarred to full consciousness, brain scrambling, I pried my eyelids open and fought to comprehend the condensed summary he was giving me, in regards to my core biopsy results.

The results, for the most part, had all come back inconclusive.

Inconclusive...as in: you stabbed me with a huge gage needle to withdraw tissue, not once but three times...ran all your tests, got the results back lickety-split...and yet you still do not know if the tumors growing within my right breast are malignant or not...?

Inconclusive. Okay, it wasn't that bad. I could deal with this. "Inconclusive? That means it could be nothing. Right?" I interrupted; half insisted.

As he began speaking again, this time I could have sworn he was hem-hawing. Or maybe he was just contemplating his own words...? Who knows? It could have just been me. Without coffee, my brain was still trapped somewhere in murky limbo, so I wasn't processing this overload of new information—let alone the medical jargon being thrown at me *(as I'd mentioned, he'd told me that because I was a nurse he would cut through the normal BS. Meaning toss out the fluff and speak to me on the level)*. It, however, was way too early *(for me anyway)*, and I wasn't fully awake quite yet. So I simply clung to the one word that my brain had instantly recognized—had had time to interpret. Inconclusive.

He had said the results had come back inconclusive...right? Which, in my mind, just meant that there was nothing really to worry about. Well at least that's how I wanted to interpret it. Okay. Wonderful. Thanks.

Now let me go back to sleep and we'll discuss this whole thing about needing surgery AFTER I've had some coffee, and if at all possible during regular business hours...nighty-night.

That scenario sounded great in theory, in my mind.... But, it wasn't on the agenda today.

There was a brief pause of hesitation, and then he finally answered my question with, "Inconclusive, yes. However, the pathologist did note a small area of necrotic cells in one of the samples. It could be nothing. But we need to go ahead with the lumpectomy to be certain."

Necrotic cells, in layman's terms: dead cells. This fact disturbed me more than the prospect of more surgery, as the samples taken were from the core of the tumor(s) itself (hence the name core biopsy). So the big question now was: Why on earth would there be dead cells smack dab in the middle of a growing tumor? Again, I knew the answer to that riddle...I just didn't want to hear the answer. So I simply did not ask.

When I didn't say anything, Dr. Beckley broke the brief lull of silence himself. "Necrotic cells are—"

"Dead cells," I croaked, finishing his own sentence for him. Dead cells, of which, were not supposed to be hanging out in the middle of living tissue...although I did not voice this opinion.

Once again as if reading my mind, he again assured me that this finding did not necessarily mean that tumor was malignant. It was however odd—suspicious...highly suspicious—and so this was why they would need to do surgery. Open me up. Remove the tumors and do a full blown biopsy. Wonderful...fucking ducky.

Defeat sunk within me like an anvil. "When?" I simply asked, referring to when this surgery would take place.

"I'm looking at this afternoon." —Okay, now I have to admit that that right there was way worse than the previously used right now from the other day, and caused my heart to stop, jump up into my throat, before settling back in place just to thump in triple time against my ribcage. Nope, I didn't need coffee anymore to kick-start my brain. I was now wide awake.— "I'm in between surgeries and I've been trying to book a suite as we speak, but they're pretty much filled up. So, if not today...first thing Monday morning. My nurse will be contacting you as soon as we know."

With that, we ended our call. Rather sardonically, I glanced toward the ceiling and muttered aloud, "You have impeccable timing, Murphy."

See, Murphy and me? Well, we go way back. It's a love-hate relationship. Murphy, he lurks in the shadowy wings of my life; just waiting for the most opportune moment to make his cameo appearance. And then, like clockwork, every single time my life happens to be going grand and in the direction I want *(perfect example: having just graduated from the nursing program, already interviewing a second time for an awesome position and eager to start my new career, just waiting to sit for the NCLEX exam in order to get my license etcetera etcetera)* well, Murphy *(A.K.A Murphy's Law: if it can go wrong it will)* just has to step in, take over, and run everything amuck.

He does this, I swear, just to test my ability to cope with...well, with whatever stressful disruption he can come up with. I'm actually beginning to believe this Murphy must view me as a worthy opponent, because—and despite the fact that I've proven myself proficient at finding my way out of his obstacle course while handling the stress he's thrown at me from every direction imaginable, time and time again—he just keeps coming back to force me to play this little sadistic game of his.

Damn him! Even though I do admit I am the type that does love a good challenge, works well under pressure....I'm just really starting to hate him.

Man, what a way to wake up. Bad news served without coffee. By now I had already bypassed bitchy mood, and was just plain pissed....and it wasn't even 8:00AM yet.

Journal Entry August 6th 2008

Another restless night. After pacing a rut in my living room, I now sit yet again staring at a blinking cursing...so I do the only thing I can. I write.

How on earth did I miss a call from Dr. Beckley's office today?! I never heard my phone ring, I swear. But there it was and I'd noticed it after the fact. At 6:00pm I'd noticed that I'd missed a call from Medical Associates.

There was a voice message.

The actual call was placed, and the message left at around 4:00pm—ish. How on earth had I missed that call?!?

Holding my breath, I listened to the message. It was again Dr. Beckley himself. The actual message was short and brief: "Deena, Dr. Beckley...Ah...? Need to speak with you. Okay, well, I'll try again...ah, if not tonight then in the morning."

The message was void of information concerning the biopsy results themselves, yet had a vague nuance of urgency to it. The undertone, although nothing was disclosed, was unsettling. Panicked, I dialed Medical Associates, and then snapped my cell phone shut. Nobody would be there at six o'clock in the evening. The offices were all closed.

Flipping my cell phone open again, I checked my settings. Mainly the ring tone volume. Placing it on the highest setting there was, I then stuffed my cell phone inside of my pocket. Then took it out again and set it right in front of me so I could see it. I stared it, waiting for Dr. Beckley to call. I did this, sat there staring at my phone, for over an hour...just waiting; mentally willing the damn thing ring.

It never did...ring that is, the rest of the evening...

So now, I sit and wonder. Stare at the clock...still waiting.

CHAPTER 3

Thursday August 7th, 2008
(eleven days after my lumpectomy)

Today, Michael *(my middle son)* leaps from childhood to teenager. It is a considerable milestone. We *(we being me, Ashley, JD, grandma and grandpa)* have sort of a surprise pizza party in the works—well JD has no knowledge of this himself, as he is only 2 and a half years old. My mom had suggested *Pizza Ranch*. I however told her *Happy Joe's*...mainly because Michael loves spending his time, and grandpa's money, in the game room.

Oh, wait....better yet, we could all drive down to Davenport and go to that one place...what the hell was the name? Michael's Fun World, wasn't it? Hmmmm...fitting. I knew that it had a massive game room...hell, the way Michael described it *(he had been there a few years back during a Boy Scout sleepover)* the whole place was a massive game room.

That place is awesome, mom! Can we go sometime? Can we, can we? Sounds like a plan to me. Sure why not...

It never did happen. Us going there, my three kids and

I as a family. I blame that on being a single parent in college; too busy to breath and always too broke. Wow, had I really sacrificed all the little things, like that, these past three years? We used to go roller-skating, to the park, out to lunch...it all stopped when I went back to college. Shameful...no just plain inexcusable, I now thought. Wanting to better provide for my kids, in turn I had become 'always too busy'; too focused on preparing for clinical rotations and studying....and let's not forget so broke I couldn't pay attention. But they knew, understood that I, their mom, was managing our household single-handed; juggling everything to somehow keep that 'everything' in some semblance of balance. Some balance....HA! In doing so, I had sacrificed the fun time....it became nonexistent.

Well, no more! I had already sacrificed three years. I was done with college now. So I decided, from this day forward my goal was to once again have fun with my kids. I would start this mission today, by taking my son, my family, to Michael's Fun World to celebrate Michael's birthday.

With that grand idea, I slipped back into the abyss of slumber. No...No...No...get up! Must get up, must get moving. I know I know....just another five minutes. Ugh....did I set the coffee maker for auto-start? Crap, probably not. I always forget. I really should get up. Need coffee....lots of it. And I still have to wrap his gifts. Wonder if I have paper? And although I had told my mom yesterday that it'd be easier to just pick up a cake from Hy-Vee....laying their cocooned in my tomb of sheets and comforter, I right then decided that I would instead bake a cake and decorate it all up for him like I used to. After all, this was a special day for Michael. He was turning the big 13.

Okay....so let's see:

* Son's birthday today...check.

* Need to buy cake--correction, get your ass up out of

bed and bake a cake for him....check.

* Presents....wait, did I buy presents? Oh, yeah...I did....just have get your butt moving GET UP and wrap them...check.

* Food....oh, right...duh....a surprise trip to Michael's Fun World.....check.

* Wrapping paper.....wrapping paper? .....have no clue. Wait, there's leftover Christmas paper....mmmm, no couldn't use that. Hey, what about a gift bag? ...isn't there a few of them in the closet, somewhere....but where?....nevermind, think about it later....

What else....? What the hell am I forgetting?...something....how about sleep?....yes, sleep is good....

My mind swirled with plans and ideas as I teeter-tottered between sleep and almost but not quite yet conscious. See, somehow my subconscious will begin running through the tasks I need to accomplish if/when a big day is at hand....well, I guess to light a fire under my lazy brain while enticing my butt to arouse from its much beloved slumber. Wait, I think I meant that the other way around.....nevermind, you get the picture.

You see, I am a bona fide night owl. I usually stay up to the wee hours, mostly writing. Writing, that's one of my hobbies (actually it's my passion). Playing medal of honor (mohaa for short) online (it's an army game), is another hobby. Once the kids go to bed and I do not have to be a mommy...well, that's my me time. I spend this me time either writing, playing mohaa, or whatever I find myself doing, before I myself turn in. Don't know why, but I learned long ago that my body and mind will not rest before the hour of eleven. I've tried, trust me. Just can't. Therefore, I cannot even try to sleep until after eleven. So getting to bed between midnight and 1:00AM...well, I run on about five to maybe six hours of sleep a night....sometimes less, especially if I happen to find myself within what I call my 'writing zone'....or just having a blast playing mohaa.

Although, during the past three years (from August 2005 through mid-July 2008), I was strictly focused on college. Instead of spending my nightly 'me' time weaving fictional tales of criminal suspense and romance, I sacrificed my hobbies and stayed up studying, cramming for exams, and/or just feverishly completing those most dreaded care-plans (required for clinical rotations). Either way, I stayed up into the wee hours of the morning....and most nights didn't turn in until 2:00 or sometimes 3:00AM, and just to get back up between the god awful hours of 5:00 and 6:00AM to start my day all over again.

Funny thing: while in college, I would awake to the little voice within my head going over what I had to accomplish that day while also reciting lab values, medical terminology, pharm equations, drug names and all the possible interactions....or whatever we happened to be learning that week. It was worse if cramming for an exam. I'd then awake to that little voice within my head drilling me with medical questions and me answering them-- aloud, no less.

Another side note: if/when I find myself in my 'writing zone' while working on a manuscript, the same damn thing happens. My brain is busily working out plotlines and dialog; that is what I awake to when that happens.

Strange....huh? Now I do admit that yes, this all sounds crazy, I know. But it's just me. A small glimpse of how I tick. With that said, let us get back to August 7th 2008.

Now that the grueling demands of the nursing program were behind me *(Although I was actually striving to acquire my RN, I exited out of the program and graduated at the LPN level due to the stress of my mother's cancer having come back. Just another shining example of Murphy strikes again)*, I could once again sleep in—well, a little bit. I still stayed up late, as I mentioned, can't go to bed before eleven—however this me time of mine was now spent reviewing for as well as cramming for NCLEX the state nursing exam. So, I'd usually wake up reciting anything and everything pertaining to nursing.

Today however was a special occasion, hence the reason behind why my brain was going over all of these birthday plans as I slowly surfaced from my state of blissful slumber.

Should I buy candles? Or would he find that childish? After all he's a teenager today. Oh my God....he is a teenager. Now I'll have two teenagers (my daughter Ashley is 16). Two of them....Lord help me! Oh, I know, I'll pick up the ones....you know, that go out but then relight. Aren't they called trick candles? Michael would love that!

Amendment: Buy trick candles....check. Crap, I still need a birthday card too.....ugh....and something else....what the hell am I forgetting????? Shut up already will you? I need quietness....just sleep!

Now like I mentioned, this whole process of going through this mental checklist and debating things with the little voice within my head, only happens if/when my body/brain knows it's an important day. Otherwise I am dead to the world. Good luck even getting me up before 7:00 or sometimes even 8:00AM, that is if my toddler allows me to sleep in. This morning, JD was being cooperative. My human alarm clock, JD, wakes around 7:00AM every morning. So on the off chance he lets me sleep in until 8:00AM or later, you'd better believe I seize it.

Out of curiosity, I allowed one eyelid to break its seal—but just a smidgen...a slit wide enough to squint one-eyed at the alarm clock stationed atop my night stand. 7:50—ish something; almost 8:00AM. I then stilled the mental checklist long enough take note of the hushed hum of the baby monitor. JD was fast asleep still. Sweet. One more hour JD...just give mommy one more hour of oblivion. I rolled over and buried my face against the coolness of my pillow while covering my head with my comforter. Power snooze....*yeeeees*. Right about that time, my cell phone began to croon—Carlos Santana's *Smooth*, filled the bedroom.

Crap.... I knew it. I just knew it! It was too good to be true. Debating on whether or not to even answer, I surrendered. Reaching for my phone, I figured I might as well get up and out of bed, as it was apparent I was not going to be allowed that extra hour to just lay there and go through my mental checklist while teetering between oblivion and snooze.

"Hello?" I answered, sitting up and flinging both sheets and comforter aside. See that way I'd already have broken the coziness of my cocoon and be forced to get up.

"Deena. Akin Beckley...." No rush. No ambush of medical jargon laced with vital information, like from before, to buttonhole my eardrum. Just my name, his, and then a splinter of hesitation.

"Yes," was automatic, as I involuntarily acknowledged my new awareness of this doctor's first name aloud. It was good start at least. No coffee, remember? So me even recognizing his first name, was well a minor feat on my score card.

After all, I had not spoken to him in person since having the lumpectomy, which I was pretty much already recovered from. Having been stressed over his whole drop-everything-and-come-in-right-now tempo, I have to admit I was a little relieved that after my lumpectomy, that hurry-up-rush-rush pace of his had stopped. My life was once again back to normal *(well whatever normal is)*.

"Good morning," I greeted, atypically stoked. For not being a morning person, for the most part, I was awake (still no coffee, remember?), and was actually eager to get up, down some java, and just get busy. My mission: to make this the most spectacular birthday my son Michael had ever anticipated.

I was also a bit thrilled to hear back from this man in general. I had given up finding out anything regarding my pathology results after calling his office damn near every day last week. I figured since it was taking this long, that

that meant it had to be good. Had to be nothing. I had pushed the entire ordeal and its ugly possibilities to farthest reaches of my mind. Because, in spite of everything, eleven days had passed since the surgery. The tumors themselves had been removed. Great, so let's move on. I had, and since I had not heard from anybody regarding results, I had basically dismissed any and all further possibilities. After all, I had a life to live and was busy living it. I had pretty much already moved on.

Denial is a grand thing. And, at this particular moment in my life, was still in my corner working overtime. Because I had received, but had also missed, a phone call from his office yesterday late afternoon. Although the message he'd left was vague and not very informative, it had at first set me on edge. But then denial kicked back in, and I figured I would just call him back the next morning.

Which was today....this morning.....shit, that's the something that I was forgetting!

When he did not speak, let alone acknowledge my greeting, a peculiar entity seemed to seep through the receiver; as tangible and as suffocating as a wet woolen blanket. And although he'd only so far managed to state my name and his, I now recognized that the quality of his voice was slightly different. Void of animation; no cheery disposition. Just a perfect blend of...well what sounded like sheer exhaustion and anguish, garnished with a pinch of graveness, a dash of remorse.

Dr. Beckley, I could now tell, was having great difficulty imparting whatever it was he had intended to share with me via this phone call. *Shit....shit, shit!*

"Yes—?" I stated and questioned simultaneously, to both assure him that it was me, that he was indeed speaking to and to also prompt him to start spilling his guts.

Although in all reality it was only mere seconds as I waited for him to say—well something, anything—those seconds seemed to linger. The hushed tick-tock of the clock, the morning chorus of songbirds, a dog barking, became a deafening buzz that bounced off my eardrums. Yet another second slipped past. Tick-tock. Tick-tock. Then absolute silence consumed the atmosphere. It was as if the entire Universe itself had paused.

This was the eerie calm before the storm, I knew.

Realizing it, I braced myself, shut my eyes, held my breath and waited those mere seconds out; half-heartedly praying that this gloomy stillness was due to my cell phone having had dropped our connection.

No such luck.

His dismal sigh foreshadowed my fate and was ensued by only two words. New words, mind you, but words which my brain could fully appreciate, yet could not quite calculate, or get a grasp on. Words that managed to unravel my once neatly woven future, leaving it—me, my life, my very existence—in a precarious tangle of frayed and dangling, loosely knotted, threads.

All of this done within the blink of an eye and with only two words: "....it's cancer."

I'm not sure how long I sat there, Indian-style, in the middle of my queen sized bed; petrified. The significance of those two words had left my mind grappling and had rendered me speechless. But Dr. Beckley must have sensed this as he empathized. Yet he did so without saying another word. He simply waited it out, patiently; allowing me the time to digest it—this...this devastating news— without once interrupting the process.

When I was able to find my voice, "Okay," was my only reply. Strangely enough that came across cool, calm and collected. No debate. Just okay.

"Deena, I need you to come into the office as soon as possible today."

"Okay," I parroted. It seemed to be the only word in my vocabulary. In all truth, it was the only word, of which I could form and push passed my lips; the only one that would fit around the thick knot of terror lodged inside my throat.

As he gave me more instructions, each time I awarded him with that same: *"okay"*. It had to be getting old by now. But it was the only word my brain would allow me to say. Maybe, just maybe if I said it enough times, I would wake up from this nightmare and everything would be *okay...?*

"I'll see you then."

Having set a time for us to meet and go over the pathology report in person, my brain picked up on the hint that he was now ready to end the call. I nodded and again said, "Okay," but then I also added something more. Odd. Not a 'I'll see you then', or 'goodbye'—no, instead I actually heard myself say to this man, "Thank you."

It did not dawn on me until after I'd flipped my phone shut, that in ending that brief call myself, I had thanked him. Had I actually just thanked him? Yep, sure as shit I had. I laughed out loud at myself. For the life of me I could not fathom why I had thanked this doctor for delivering such devastating news...?

...it's cancer. Okay. Thank you...

As the minutes ticked passed I just sat there. No tears. No fit of rage. No annoying little voice mocking me anymore because of that *"thank you"*. Not even the inkling of a thought passed through my brain. I didn't even twitch a muscle. Void of any and all emotion, I had simply shut down; shut everything out and off. And so I just sat, Indian-style atop my bed, staring at my own reflection via the dresser's mirror....for once in my life, at a complete and utter loss.

CHAPTER 4

August 7th 2008 *(The longest appointment of my life)*

My mind, still sheltered by denial, was left in a state of stunned disbelief. In effect, I was in shock. My brain had simply flipped the main switch—had shut down everything except basic life-support, forcing me to muddle through my typical morning rituals on autopilot. The only three things I somehow managed to do somewhat competently was wake JD, make coffee and call my parents.

My mother came over immediately and, as I just sat there in a blank stupor, made JD breakfast, bathed and dressed him to get him ready for preschool/daycare. We dropped him off then drove to Medical Associates. Neither of us spoke. In shock still, I had become a mute. But I think my mother understood this. Together we met with Dr. Beckley as scheduled (although I do not recall the exact time now. 10am-ish?). Sullen faced, he gave me a copy of the pathology report. I scanned it—but had no clue what I was supposed to do with it. The neatly typed words all looked so foreign. As he informed me that the mass he had removed during my lumpectomy, had been attached to the muscle of my chest wall, he seemed so...well, sad and apologetic. He assured me that if he had indeed known, he would have taken more.

Not understanding, I blankly stared at him, nodded, and again said, "Okay..."

Although this information seemed to be quite upsetting to him as well as my mom, my brain was still on complete lockdown; therefore, I did not grasp the implication of why it was so worrisome within the grand scope of things. I chose to simply translate it as: yes, the tumors were cancerous and they had been removed. Okay. Great. Enough chitchat. What's next? Let's get this party started and be done with it. What mattered to me right then and there was what we needed to do, how soon it was all going to happen, and mainly how long this would all take. After all, I was a busy mom with three children to raise, a household to manage, and let's not forget that new career I so eagerly wanted to get started. *(You see, I had already had a second interview with the Dixon Correctional Facility. Before I could be officially hired, however, I first had to sit for the Iowa NCLEX and pass then obtain my IL LPN endorsement. While waiting for the big okay to take my NCLEX, I had already started the boatload of paperwork to request my Illinois endorsement...a major headache, but I wanted that awesome LPN position with its kick-ass pay and sweet benefits package.)*

Because he was my surgeon we mainly discussed-- in depth—the necessity of having a mastectomy; what that surgery itself would entail/involve and also talked about a double mastectomy (removing both breasts). Statistics have proven that it is common for this type of cancer to come back—yet again—in the unaffected breast within five years. Therefore, Dr. Beckley was proposing that the most logical thing to do was to have both breasts removed—simple prevention to avoid reoccurrence.

Both—? The idea itself was...well, to be totally honest it was a bit alarming. Yet, on the medical aspect, I could see the logic. However off the wall, I agreed that it was the right thing to do. There was no way in hell I wanted to go through what I had just gone through within the past few days, weeks, all over again! Although I did hate the idea, I thought *fine, remove both and let's just be done with this!* At this point anger began to simmer—a low rolling boil, cueing my brain to summon the only ally of which it knew of, that would permit me to cope. Humor. Raw, uninhibited, borderline sarcastic, some claim sadistic, razor sharp wit. Twisted, yes, I know...but, hey whatever works, right...?

Faced with losing not one but both breasts, I suddenly clutched mine protectively and blurted, "Wait...I get new boobs. Right?" Mind you, I'm sitting atop the exam table in one of those stupid paper exam gowns, my chest now thrust out as if to better show him 'my girls' within my hands. "Because I've had these babies for a while now, doc—sorta used to them—even though they are a pain in the ass. So if you're gonna just go chopping 'em both off, you are going to be replacing them....correct?" I paused for effect, then snorted before rambling on with, "My God, these things are huge—hell, always wanted a reduction. So the new ones, they don't have to be this big. I don't know, what do you think? Something like a nice perky B, maybe a firm C cup?"

Bam. Bam. Bam. Just like that.

Tongue now in cheek, Dr. Beckley had halted mid-sentence. My own mother's jaw had dropped, literally. Glancing between the two, my gaze rested on my mom's and I was not sure if she was going to break down in tears from sheer embarrassment or just bust a gut laughing. Either way, my out of the blue and rather uncensored outburst—however trivial in the scope of things—had dissolved the tension.

"Well...yes," Dr. Beckley began, rather carefully. Looking first at my mother then back at me, an involuntary grin twitched, and then blossomed. Finally, that famous jovial disposition of his was back. "Most women, your age, opt to have reconstructive surgery—" Hesitating, he then beamed at me and in afterthought announced, "I like this attitude, Deena. Keep it."

I smiled back, and gave him a what-are-you-going-to-do shrug then pondered the idea of new breasts. Wow. What an upshot! My once gloomy day had just become a smidgen brighter. I could for sure deal with this. "Okay...but will my insurance pay for them?" I asked, somewhat suspicious. New boobs. I mean seriously, it just sounded too good to be true. There had to be a catch *(I just did not know at that particular moment what that 'catch' was yet)*.

"Yes. In this case, insurance covers reconstructive surgery," he assured me then further went on to explain the several different surgical procedures available in regards to reconstruction itself. He was now beginning to sound as excited as I felt.

Tram-flap. Expansion with implants; either saline or silicon, your pick...etcetera, etcetera. Wow, who knew there were so many options and choices? Either way it all equated to one thing. Brand new breasts! I probed further, after all talking about getting new boobs was way better than discussing some stupid pathology report.

"Cool...So I'll get new boobs right away," I stated almost as if to confirm it. After all, who wouldn't want new boobs?

"Yep," he nodded. "Well, they'll start the expansion process anyway. It takes—"

"Sweet. So when I'm like ninety years old, I'll still have perky twenty-year-old ta-tas."

"Pretty much," he chuckled.

"So how soon can we do this?"

"Well...they can start the expansion process at the same time as the mastectomies. It will take about three to four months to stretch the tissue before they can—"

"Awesome!" I interrupted yet again. I was so hyped at the idea I was by now grinning from ear to ear *(thinking about it now, I probably sounded like a babbling nitwit quizzing him about the process of the reconstructive surgery itself as he was himself trying to explain it).*

"Sweet... I can deal with this," I announced to both my mother and Dr. Beckley.

Strange how when a person is faced with something so horrific, their mind latches on to what appears to be that glimmer of a silver lining.

After a quick exam to check my lumpectomy incision, Dr. Beckley referred me to a plastic surgeon in the Quad Cities (who specializes in reconstructive surgery). We then discussed when I would be having this proposed double mastectomy and once again I got that already famous: *as soon as possible* from him. Which, strangely enough, in this case I was thrilled. In my mind, I was thinking that the sooner I had the double mastectomy that not only would this all be done and over with, but the sooner I would be getting my new boobs. Before we could set an actual date for my upcoming surgery, he informed me that I would first have to meet with Dr. Aggarwal, an oncologist.

Dr. Beckley had arranged for me to meet with him as well, in regards to setting up a treatment plan or something. Yeah, sure, great, okay...now let's get back to discussing my new boobies....okay?

We did. And I was told that I would have to first meet with the plastic surgeon he'd referred me to, and then he would himself have to confer with him while also arrange to do his part (my double mastectomy surgery) in the Quad Cities due to the fact that this particular plastic surgeon did not perform reconstructive surgeries in Clinton. Which was fine by me as I did not care if we had to drive to tin-buck-two...I was going to be getting new boobs!

Wrapping things up, he gestured for a high-five—a gesture that fostered our doctor/patient partnership. Now mind you, it is a rather unorthodox handshake but I was used to this and knew exactly what to do. High-five, clasp hands, fingers intertwined half above our heads (a display of victory I suppose) then a brief half hug with a pat on the shoulder in a show of encouragement (just another cool characteristic of this doctor, of which I enthusiastically conformed to and liked about him).

While doing this handshake of ours, he told me in parting, "Awesome attitude, Deena. Keep it." Although my mind was still swimming with an overload of information, and I had really no clue why he was saying it, I promised him that I would. After all, this awesome surgeon had just promised me a pair of new boobs.

I coasted on that new sense of excitement as I met Dr. Aggarwal, my new oncologist. Mind you, this same oncologist had been treating my mother. He had referred her case to Iowa City, however was still within the loop in regards to her treatment. So needless to say, we went through another 'oh, this is your daughter?' routine yet again. This time around, however, it just was not as comical to watch as it had been with Dr. Beckley.

Don't get me wrong, Dr. Aggarwal is good in all respects at what he does. Extremely knowledgeable. He too has a wonderful bedside manner. He is more reserved and quiet...and, well, just more of a let's-get-down-to-business type of doctor.

I of course had to go through yet another exam. As this new doctor scrutinized me from head to toe, all I could talk about was the reconstructive surgery. He of course entertained me, and while talking about my recent decision to undergo a double mastectomy he also briefly explained the whole reconstructive process himself. He even made my day when he poked my belly and mentioned something about being too skinny while questioning if I had enough tissue for what he called a tram-flap. After my exam however, when he came back into the room...well, he now had full intentions of discussing the pathology report as well as his proposed treatment plan.

Man...what a killjoy! I still wanted to talk about my new boobs.

Not only did he explain, in depth, the severity...he then had to go and diagnose me with Stage III-B Invasive Ductal Carcinoma, with triple negatives. My new oncologist was hell-bent on making sure I fully understood that not only did I have one of the deadliest forms of breast cancer there was, but that the mass itself had already begun to spread! It had already rooted to the muscle of my chest wall. In addition, the report also stated that it had permeated the lymph and vascular systems. Furthermore, even though they had removed the tumors—now dubbed the mass—they were uncertain to whether or not they had removed it all...

The pathology report: The mass is seen to involve grossly the resection margin...

This was what Dr. Beckley had been trying to tell me earlier; felt he needed to apologize for. See...when a surgeon removes a tumor (or mass) for a biopsy, they normally just take the tumor itself. It is a simple procedure; outpatient surgery. When they indeed already know that a mass is malignant, it becomes a more complicated and involved surgical procedure. Not only do they take the mass, they also take a certain amount of good tissue surrounding the mass itself (called a margin) just to make certain they've removed any and all trace of possible cancer cells that might be hidden and/or lurking about undetected.

Now, nobody—and I mean nobody—could have ever foreseen that the mass growing within me was indeed cancerous, let alone the type it was (we only had suspicion, hence the need for the biopsy itself), not to mention that it had already attached itself to the muscle of my chest wall. Therefore, Dr. Beckley simply was not surgically prepared to slice and dice up my chest wall while removing the mass itself.

He performed a lumpectomy. In effect, that is what I had signed permission for. Although after opening me up and seeing that the mass had attached itself, he did what he could do at the time...he removed the tumors for biopsy, as well as took only a small margin of the muscle tissue itself. In retrospect, I feel he did not need to apologize. I mean it is not like it was his fault. He didn't know. And, it's not like this stuff is color coded, or has some wall type map smack dab in the middle of it to point out: you are here...and we're right there, and here, oh and there, by the way, we just sent a few feeler cells just west of here to scope out the lymphatic system...now that's prime real-a-state there...

So, in other words, it was highly probably that there was still cancerous cells left to grow rampant within the muscle of my chest wall. Therefore, I would not be having that double mastectomy with reconstructive surgery, just yet. Nope, my oncologist had other plans. First, he wanted a PET scan (as soon as possible) in order to see exactly how far this cancer had spread. Due to the aggressive nature as well as the advanced stage, Dr. Aggarwal felt that it was crucial that I start chemotherapy pronto.

Hearing this, my recent enthusiasm over my new boobies was ripped from my grasp. Blindsided by this most recent information...well, to tell you the truth it was as brutal as a harsh slap. Mind grappling, I was stunned...once again so dumbfounded I was rendered speechless. Petrified, I stared at my mother who was herself looking alarmed, wide-eyed, and in a state of sheer panic. Due to my own inability to speak, she began her own rapid-fire interrogation.

Her main inquiry: What is her prognosis?

Dr. Aggarwal again explained that this was not just a simple case of breast cancer. This was classified as Stage III-B Advanced Breast Cancer. Worse, due the aggressive nature and it having that 'triple negatives' tag (meaning the cancer cells themselves had no favorable receptors, therefore would not respond to the various hormonal therapy drugs available for combating it) statistically, my chances of survival was a grim 50%.

Wait....what—? Back the hell up! Are you saying: I could...well, that I might...well, you know...die—? As in take the eternal nap, pushing up roses, six feet under, dead? Dead, dead? As in cease to exist therefore not be alive to raise my kids and start that new career of mine? And all because of...well, this...this, it wasn't there six months ago but magically just appeared overnight poof-here-I-am lump—correction, mass of mine? The one you guys just removed? Mind you, these were just the thoughts now racing through my head.

I—right along with my mother—was floored.

Offered the option of seeking a second opinion, I choked back what would have been a hoarse sardonic cackle. By the sounds of it, there really was no time for debating, or second guessing this. Dr. Aggarwal excused himself so that my mother and I could have a moment to ourselves. I assumed he had done this, so that we could both collect ourselves as well as discuss the option of seeking a second opinion in private.

While my mother voiced her views out loud, I shut my eyes, blocked everything out and hastily weighed my options. One: I could breakdown right then and there, ball myself up into a fetal position and just let fate run its course. Or two: I could face this head-on...and at least go out kicking, swinging, and screaming at the top of my lungs. Either way, seeking a second opinion wasn't going to do me much good. My fate was neatly typed out in black ink upon the pathology report itself.

Stage III-B Invasive Ductal Carcinoma; triple negatives. Prognosis: Unfavorable... I, literally, did not have the luxury of time on my side for seeking a second opinion.

Taking a deep breath I looked at my new oncologist as he returned and asked him point-blank, "What's our game plan?"

Asking that very question, I quickly found myself once

again in a blur of mass confusion. It was as if everybody was coming at me from every direction. First to Cardiology for an echocardiogram—they needed to know whether or not my heart could take the harsh chemotherapy drugs they would be starting me on. A debate to whether they could start this chemo via a simple IV. No, no...just too harsh. So yet another meeting with Dr. Beckley and his primary nurse to discuss as well as set a time for my port placement surgery. Then it was off to the lab for full panel work-up...then yet again back to Aggarwal's office for yet more tests, discussions, debates, and instructions. Then a quick tour, as well as a 'meet and greet' the nurses in the chemo lab...and so on and so forth.

Ensnared in a befuddled daze, I simply agreed to and underwent every test and procedure they'd ordered for me that day; numbly going along and doing as instructed without question. My mind had dislodged itself from all logic. I kept trying to tell myself this was not happening. My mom was sitting in the waiting room in tears; calling my dad, my sister, anybody and everybody she could think of, to explain to them what was happening.

Poked and prodded and examined a dozen or so times now, I seriously began to believe that if I could just pinch myself; slap myself; shake myself hard enough—my God somebody do something!—maybe this would all cease. All the while, a tiny little voice from somewhere deep inside of me kept chanting louder and louder, "Wake up! Just wake the hell up!"

But, I was already awake; now trapped within this nightmare, my new reality.

The game plan was set:

1) PET scan scheduled for the next morning, Friday August 8th.

2) Port placement surgery scheduled for the following Monday morning August 11th.

3) Begin chemotherapy Tuesday, August 12th, bright and early at 8:30AM.

Bam. Bam. Bam. Just like that.

A nurse from the chemo lab handed me a piece of paper with this information written upon it, then ushered me back into an exam room to yet again speak with my oncologist. I was beginning to believe this day would never end.

"Do you have any questions for me?" was all Dr. Aggarwal had wanted to ask me.

I stared at him blankly and then almost laughed out loud. *Sure do, doc. Answer me this...Why me? Why now? Why!?* Instead, I simply shook my head no. The questions I had where ones he would not have any answers to, anyhow.

I was sent home with an arm-load of pamphlets and instructions. An Understanding Breast Cancer booklet; information about the two chemotherapy drugs that they were going to pump in to me, the risks, a brief rundown of possible side-effects—blah blah blah....and, last but not least, instructions in preparation for the PET scan. A special diet for supper, and then afterward no food and or liquids after 9:00PM.

By this time, both my mother and I were exhausted. We had just spent the entire day at Medical Associates. It was already after 4:00PM. I was beyond overwhelmed. My friend Denial had split. Numbness filled the void. Still, there were no tears. I couldn't cry. I was in shock. While my brain remained on autopilot, all rational logic was jarred off course and I was now lost somewhere between the murky realm of mass confusion and just plain scared shitless.

Do you have any questions for me...?

The very question we'd ended our long day with drifted above the buzz of chaos cluttering my head. At the time he'd asked, I couldn't even think straight let alone form a question. Yet now, as my mom drove me back to my own house, only one question surfaced. *How on earth do I tell my three kids?*

CHAPTER 5

August 8th 2008 *(Pre-admit for port placement surgery and the PET scan)*

Bleary eyed, I pulled into Mercy Medical Center's lot and parked. I first had to meet with the pre-admit nurse to go over and sign all the paperwork necessary for my upcoming port placement surgery. Oh joy. No coffee, no breakfast, hardly any sleep, and I wasn't sure if this nurse was also going to have a go at me—as in scrutinize me from head to toe herself, as well.

In all truth, I was more anxious over what they would find during the PET scan. Regardless, this masked itself as annoyance as anger still simmered just below the surface— which had somehow upgraded itself overnight to bubble within me like molten lava looking for an escape route.

"Isn't it splendid? Why I have half a mind to do this all outside," the pre-admit nurse exclaimed.

Okay...so the weather was nice. Beautiful in fact. Amazingly, not yet suffocating hot (which is the usual temp for August in Iowa.) Blue sky as far as the naked eye could see, not a stitch of cloud in sight, allowing sunshine to sparkle out the wazzoo. Big deal. I didn't care as I had other things on my mind. And so I stared at this seasoned nurse with an expression of sheer incredulity. Nothing felt, let alone remotely resembled splendid in my new world of muddied uncertainty.

I survived her excessively chipper—to the point of being faux—personality, even stomached her expressed pity. Nobody really knows what to say, I don't think. Reactions run the gambit from stupid shock, aghast, to tears and outrage. Today it was pity and something on the lines of oh-so-sad-so-young-isn't-that-shame. After explaining the port-placement procedure, giving me my pre-surgery instructions and gathering my information, she escorted me to the main reception area and spoke to the elderly volunteer at the desk *(who I guess was a breast cancer survivor herself, or knew of somebody who was....still not sure of that myself).* Anyway, this elderly volunteer gave me a business card and pamphlet for a local breast cancer support group. She then took me to the PET scan reception area itself.

Despite the fact that it was rather warm outside, following the instructions given to me the day before, I had dressed comfortable and warm in a pair of sweatpants, my CCC nursing T-shirt which proclaimed on the backside: 'Be nice...I may be your nurse someday'. Which now seemed laughable, considering. I had also pulled my mid-back length hair in to a half-pony-tail-half-bun, placed smack dab atop my head with a cloth scrunchie. The receptionist scanned me from head to toe. Nothing I wore that day for the PET scan could have any metal in or on it. And, as instructed, I had left all my jewelry at home. Satisfied with my rather sloppy attire, this new woman then ushered me outside to a semi-trailer parked out back.

Now...I have to admit, this whole thing seemed...well, strange for lack of a better word. I mean, I see these semis parked here and there at different medical facilities all of the time and know exactly what they are for. But I myself have never been inside of one. So at this particular moment, the whole idea that I was going to go inside of a semi, in order to have some spectacular medical procedure done of which I knew had to cost a small fortune...well, it just seemed rather strange. Almost ludicrous, really.

Staring at this mobile PET scan unit, parked out back, I snickered at the idea.

A somewhat handsome looking man exited from a side door *(hey I was single, I noticed these things)* greeted us, and after he himself scanned me from head to toe (again for metal), he then gestured for me to join him on the Tommy type elevator lift. Skeptical, I glanced between the removable metal stairwell—of which, he had himself just jogged down. The side door he'd just exited from. *Um....can't we just go in that way, you know, via the door? The one you just came out of?* With those thoughts, I eyed him and asked, "What's wrong with those stairs?"

After all, I wasn't handicap.

"This thing's fun to use," he grinned, then after reading my hesitancy explained something about needing to lift it for a patient inside who I guess was in a wheelchair. Of course...just my luck. I again sized up the mobile unit; eyed the Tommy type lift he was now standing on and looking a bit too eager to operate. Okay, sure. What the hell. I joined him on the platform, and then held on white knuckled for dear life as the thing jerked, moaned, and then slowly defied gravity to sputter its way up.

Ironically, it would have been faster to have taken the stairs.

Once he slid open the door and I stepped inside, my jaw hit the floor. Although the quarters were rather cramped and the temp itself was on the chilly side, I was in awe at the amount of high-tech equipment and gadgetry. "Holy crap!" I muttered under my breath, then glanced at Mr. Somewhat Handsome and said, "...no wonder these scan thingies cost a small fortune...just look at this place."

"Pretty cool, huh?" he replied, obviously enjoying my

reaction.

I nodded, scanning my surroundings. This seemingly plain shell of a semi-trailer from the outside, with its questionable Tommy type lift, was loaded to the hilt on the inside. Taking in every inch of the dimly lit surroundings after he slid the door shut to seal off that sparkling sunshine, I felt as if I'd just been 'beamed up' into a futuristic stage set for some thrilling Sci-fi adventure.

That adventure started off with a brief medical history and confirmation that I had not had any food or liquids. Another man, Mr. Somewhat Handsome's partner I assumed, appeared like magic from a narrow door. After scanning my history and asking me a few questions himself, he then introduced himself—with happy flourish, I might add—as the one who would be injecting me with the 'radioactive gunk' required for the PET scan. He then also excitedly announced that I was very first patient and he couldn't wait to get started, because he'd heard that people actually glowed from this junk.

Radioactive gunk...? Comical. Playing along, I laughed, "Cool. I just graduated as a nurse, so guess we can muddle through this together," then added in question, "So I'm gonna glow huh?" instantly liking this man's warped sense of humor.

"From the inside out," he jested.

After scoping out my arms for a good vein to use, he directed me toward a second narrow door adjacent to the one he'd just come out of. Thank God I'm not claustrophobic as this narrow door slid open to a tiny square room which was about as comfortable and inviting as a port-a-potty. It was just big enough for one of those clumsy vinyl covered hospital recliner type chairs, and that was it. I literally had to back into it, and sit, as there was no room to move.

We joked more as he placed my butterfly IV—him asking me questions about my nursing; me asking him questions about his job. Once he injected this so-called 'radioactive gunk' inside me, he fled and quickly slid the door shut sealing me in total isolation—must be some pretty potent radioactive gunk. Despite the fact he'd informed he would do this, which was understandable, it was still slightly a bit too unnerving.

I studied my arm, the IV itself. Other than the actual stick of the butterfly IV, I couldn't really feel any sensation of this 'radioactive gunk' coursing throughout my veins. After a few minutes, his friendly voice filtered through a mini speaker, asking me if I was doing okay.

I looked myself over then up at the small camera watching me and replied, "Maybe it isn't working? I'm not glowing yet."

Settling in for the long haul, I simply lounged in the chair provided and read the book that I'd brought with me to pass the time. This waiting period lasted for an hour, and after inspecting myself periodically (you know, just to make sure that I wasn't glowing) I think I nodded off once or twice; despite the knowledge that a small camera was still eyeballing me the entire time (nobody really likes to be watched while drooling in their sleep....come on).

When I was done 'cooking', Mr. Comical came back and led me back into the cramped quarters of the....well, I guess the PET scan area. After a split second discussion about my bra (because it was an under-wire....no metal remember?), I was offered the option of returning to the tiny room to remove it. HA, um right....there's a camera in there, remember? Nice try but don't think so guys. To their amazement, I simply snaked my arms inside of my shirt and removed it right then and there; no fuss, no muss, no show, and handed it to Mr. Comical for safe keeping (the look on his face was priceless and we all shared a hearty laugh over it). With that out of the way, he had me hop onto the narrow table like bed that would pass me through the scanner itself. Secured to the table, strapped in from head to toe so that I couldn't move, the whole process was then started. Unlike a CAT scan and the

MRI, there really was no sound expect for a hush hum the equipment itself. For the first five minutes or so, I listened and inspected everything that I could within the range of eyeball movement....then simply closed my eyes and allowed myself to relax.

Doing so allowed my brain to wander, run through everything I knew of this PET scan procedure, cancer itself, as well as metastasis.

Metastasis is defined as: when cancerous cells break away from the tissue/organ on which they are growing and travel to other parts of the body where they continue to thrive and grow. Commonly, these cells spread to nearby internal organs (in the case of breast cancer it likes to migrate to the lungs, bones, brain, liver, or skin) after its invaded the vascular system (the bloodstream) and lymphatic system (lymph nodes)...which, as it happens, are the two very same systems of vessels that bathe and feed all of the body's organs.

Wonderful.... Since my own pathology report had suggested that my very own mass had already taken it upon itself to permeate my lymphatic and vascular systems...well, this was a major worry to me-- as it was the main reason, I was now dozing on this narrow little table being passed through some high-tech machine called a PET scanner.

My brain continued reciting the information I knew....

PET *(Positron Emission Tomography)* scan is a standard imaging tool, which allows physicians to pinpoint the location of cancer within the body. The highly sensitive scan detects the metabolic signal of actively growing cancer cells and provides a detailed picture of the internal anatomy that reveals the location, size and shape of abnormal cancerous growths. Furthermore, if/when the results of PET and CT scans are "fused" together (these two imaging tools are commonly used together as well as can be done at the same time), the combined image provides complete information on cancer location and its metabolism (how fast or slow it's growing/spreading). This is all possible because many cancer cells are highly metabolic and therefore synthesize the radioactive glucose (sugar, or as Mr. Comical had called it, 'radioactive gunk') which is injected in the patient prior to the exam. The areas of high glucose uptake are dramatically displayed in the scan imagery, pinpointing the location of active, viable tumors...

And there you have it...a basic run down of the PET scan. And the reason I know all of this? Because it was all being done to me, to see exactly how far my own cancer had spread. Ah...but where on earth did I learn the above information...?

Well, let me back up a bit....to the previous night...

You see, after returning home from the longest appointment of my life, I was still grappling over how to even tell my kids. Once home however, I realized my son Michael was already at his dad's...and wouldn't be home until Sunday night. Yeah, I know, boy did I ever tell that annoying little voice within my head how stupid it was for going through that mental checklist that morning. Sure it was my son's birthday, and my brain—I guess out of excitement of it being such a milestone—had forgotten Michael was spending his birthday with his dad.

In a way I was relieved. After all, what was I supposed to say...? Hey buddy, happy 13th birthday Mike....oh by the way, honey, mommy just found out she has cancer and might die...? Talk about a shitty birthday present! Jeesh.

So, I decided to wait until Mike returned home. Besides I was still unsure how to tell them and I also wanted to tell my kids all together (well, JD was too young to even understand any of it, thank God). Because I had to eat a special diet I was somewhat able to directly avoid my daughter's quizzical questions of why, as well as what I had found out at the doctors. Requesting she keep an eye on JD, I appeased her with the promise of allowing her best-friend to spend the night and pizza from anywhere they wanted. It seemed to stop their combined questions and satisfied her and her best-friend (another teenager, of which also called me mom, as I had figuratively speaking adopted this kid as one of my own due to her always hanging out with my daughter at our house damn near twenty-four/seven) allowing me enough time to escape their concerned expressions.

Returning home from Hy-Vee, following my special diet—a high protein/low carb meal—I cooked up my recently purchased thick juicy steak and smothered it in plain mushrooms. I added a side of green beans and cottage cheese, accompanied by a glass of ice-water. Yummy.... Actually the meal wasn't that bad. Again avoiding my daughter and her friend, I played with JD. Then after getting him ready for and in bed, I threw myself into my NCLEX review books, the entire time consuming enough plain black coffee to float the Titanic (although, could not add my usual creamer and sugar, which sucked) before 9:00PM. I guess I figured that way I'd get my fill of java (as if it would carry over into the next day), due to the fact that I could not wake up and have my much beloved go-go juice, or anything before the PET scan. After confirming that JD was fast asleep himself...at the stroke of nine sharp, I peeled off my contacts, brushed my teeth and got ready for—and then holy crap stop the presses—crawled in to my bed.

Both outrageous and hilarious, yes I know. Night owl, remember?

I guess because I knew I could not have anything to eat—which really didn't bother me that much because I am not a serial 'night snacker' myself—I figured if I just went to bed I then wouldn't be tempted to drink anything either. I have a terrible habit of drinking coffee, or sun-tea twenty-four/seven, so why chance it. Well....needless to say, me going to bed and trying to sleep at such an early hour was about as productive as somebody using their back molars to try and open a soup can. It just wasn't going to happen. So I laid there, on edge, staring at the glowing demon-red digits of my alarm clock. From somewhere upstairs (think my daughter Ashley's bedroom?), the hushed tick-tock of clock began to grade on my nerves...almost mockingly, really.

Tick....now, what the hell are you doing in bed?....Tock. It's called sleeping. You should try it. Tick....you crazy fool, you know you can't sleep unless it's after eleven!....Tock. I know, I know....but—Tick...all you're gonna do is toss and turn....Tock. If you'd shut the hell up, maybe I could—Tick....you in bed before eleven, better mark that one on the calendar, it's just absurd!....Tock.

Now in addition to this most annoying little voice, my brain was allowed to wander, and the longer I laid there I found myself stewing. I was still trying to grasp the idea that I had cancer and was now nervous over not knowing how far that cancer had spread....knew the PET scan that would give us that answer, and of course beat myself up of the fact that I still needed to find a way to break this news to my children. Tick....tock. I tossed and turned. Tick....Tock. Turned and tossed. The last straw: my bladder itself betrayed me—joining in this outright mutiny with a much unrelenting *ooooh godda-go-godda-go-godda-go and now or I'm a gonna burst!* All that coffee, remember? Yeah.

UGH! Kicking at then flinging the sheets and comforter aside, I bolted downstairs. Relief. I glanced at the bathroom clock and laughed out loud. It was only 9:30ish—something—PM.

"Um....are you alright, mom?" my own daughter quizzed, after poking her nose into the bathroom. (Kids! Nothing is private when you have kids...not even the bathroom.)

"Huh? Oh, um yeah. Fine," I fibbed, smiled and then toed at the door, hoping to reseal it before she could push it open even farther. Unsuccessful, she inched it open, to now study me a moment with a mixed expression of disbelief and suspicion.

Avoiding her prying gaze, I glanced down as one of

our cats (Oreo) squeezed through the small opening to begin winding herself between my ankles. Smart cat. Oreo does this on a regular basis, if you happen to leave the bathroom door ajar, because she knows whoever is sitting on the pot is a captive audience. You are forced to pet her. I absentmindedly stroked her tail and shot a look at my dog. Cindy—my loyal dog who is also always at my side if not under my feet—had flopped on the floor outside of the bathroom, to wait for me. She now pushed her snout within the breech that my own daughter had made at the threshold, as if to see herself what was up.

My God...did one person need so much help to pee? Did I mention, nothing is private-- including the use of the bathroom-- at my house?

"Uh-huh. Sooooo, why you in bed so early?" my daughter quizzed.

"I'm not in bed. As you can see, I am in the bathroom, sitting on the toilet. Do you mind—?" I snapped, slamming the door shut then twisting the lock in order to shelve any further debate. I then stared down at my cat Oreo and sighed an exasperated, "What—?" cueing her to paw at the closed door, wanting to escape my wrath. Poor cat.

So back to my daughter.... Avoidance. Cruel, I know. I had yet to tell my kids much of anything that had been going on. Which, had been relatively easy. They knew something was up with all of the doctor appointments...but really had no clue of what. It was summer, so the older two were lost in their own worlds. And JD, well he was too young to even know let alone understand. By now I had decided to wait until after my PET scan results to tell them. That way I would have a better picture myself and be able to share with them everything....not worry them while waiting for those results. Procrastination....okay maybe....I know. But I was still searching for the best way to tell them 'oh by the way, mommy has cancer and might die' in the first place.

So anyway.... Knowing that I wouldn't be able to sleep, and after finally coming out of hiding (exiting the bathroom itself), I holed myself up inside my office. I had spent the entire night (into the wee hours of morning) flipping through and reading from my nursing textbooks and then also surfing the net....searching for every bit of information I could find in regards to PET scans, advanced breast cancer itself, and metastasis.

Hence, the reason I began my day bleary eyed and in such a peachy mood...and probably why I was dozing throughout most of my PET scan. I awoke to Mr. Handsome peering down at me. When he asked if I wanted to put my bra back on before I left, I tried to sit up to no prevail. *HUH? Wait...what? Why am I strapped...oh yeah.* Once it dawned where I was and why, I laughed. As they provided me with one of those plastic take home hospital bags (to put my bra inside), Mr. Comical told me my oncologist would contact me in regards to the scan results. Mr. Handsome offered me another ride on the lift. I declined and took the stairs.

Famished, I jumped in my car and high-tailed it straight to *Burger King's* drive through then stuffed my face as I drove back home. Pulling into the garage, I finished my meal then checked myself via the review mirror yet again. I had survived my first PET scan, and I was not glowing. I then just sat there and stared at my reflection; now wondering if my daughter was lurking inside, waiting to ambush me with yet another round of twenty questions? I closed my eyes and pinched the bridge of my nose at the idea, uncertain myself how much longer I could keep this 'nothing is wrong, everything's fine' poker-faced facade of mine going...?

Author's note...

A phoenix is a mythical bird with a colorful plumage and a tail of gold and scarlet (or purple and blue, according to some sources). It has a 500 to 1,000 year life-cycle, near the end of which it builds itself a nest of myrrh twigs that then ignites; both nest and bird burn fiercely and are reduced to ashes, from which a new, young phoenix arises-- reborn anew to live once again. This mystical bird is also said to have the ability to regenerate if/when hurt or wounded by a foe, thus being almost immortal and invincible-- it is also said that this magical creature can heal a person with a single tear from its eye, making them temporarily immune to death...

Although the phoenix is mere fable, it's a symbol of fire and mysticism; synonymous with rebirth and/or recovery, especially after calamity...

CHAPTER 6

You gain strength, courage and confidence by every experience in which you really stop to look fear in the face... You must do the thing you cannot do. —*Eleanor Roosevelt*

Sunday August 10, 2008 *(the breaking point)*

Really wish you'd quit smoking, Dee... As my father's suggestion tumbled throughout my mind, I closed my eyes and sighed at the idea. Regardless, I lit another cigarette as I pondered our earlier conversation, mostly my own cattiness directed toward him. Fed-up, I'd unleashed that 'some claim sadistic' part of my coping mechanism (that twisted humor of mine) on my own father.

"Are you serious—? Um, hello dad. Why quit now? I already have cancer...so what's another cig? According the pathology report I'm pretty much the walking dead!"

Shock, pain and then sorrow crawled across my father's features. Though my father is a master at masking and bottling his emotions, the grief leaked through, glossing his eyes and clouding his voice as he spoke, "Was just saying is all..." He tried clearing his throat to no prevail. "This is hard on all of us, Dee. You don't have to be so catty about it...okay? I was just saying is all."

My father (a deeply emotional soul, although a stoic man of very few words) truly understood me; my coping methods. Probably because I was, in so many ways, much like him. I too had the ability to mask and bottle my emotions; keep people guessing. My father is notorious for telling the men that I get involved with: "careful, she's moody"...as he knows that I can go from being calm cool and collected to royal bitch in seconds flat, and back at the drop of a hat. This usually only happens if/when I feel threatened, or just stressed out to the max. He refers to this moody behavior of mine as being catty. He usually ignores it. And it's only on rare occasion that he voices objection to it. Occasions when he himself feels helpless and threatened; unable fix things for me, his daughter, his little girl, his baby.

This was one of those rare moments.

"Sorry. Little stressed out and I don't need—" Stopping myself short to swallow the sardonic air, I then found myself choking on a knot and blinking back the sting of tears as he gathered me up in a hug. Dammit! I rarely cry in front of anyone! My father included. Composing myself quickly, aloofness reigned suppressing my fear, my own grief. Hugging him back, I sighed hard, "I love you, dad. But please don't ask me to give up my only vice right now. Okay?"

"Me too," *(me too and/or ditto are my father's unique way of returning that 'I love you')* he replied, giving me an extra-long squeeze (proof he was pretty much scared shitless himself). "Okay, I'll try not to mention it again. But really wish you'd think about it, Dee."

Sighing as our conversation faded within my mind, I inhaled deeply then released a plume of smoke. Maybe I should? Quit that is. I'd been thinking about it; meaning to do so...and way before all of this. I knew it was unhealthy. But...it was my only vice.

Heavy hearted, ashamed at how viciously I'd snapped at my father earlier, and without warrant, I crushed out my cigarette. I wasn't mad at him directly. It was just...I was so angry over this whole thing itself. Still, there was no excuse. And I now felt like an ass for even letting myself unleash my fury in such a raw brutal manner over a simple suggestion. It seemed I was doing that—snapping at random comments a lot lately. It was almost like a pressure release valve would momentarily allow short burst to leak out in order to contain the mounting tension within me. Involuntarily done to save what was left of my sanity.

I was losing my grip. HA! My handle on life itself had broke. All the while, I was still stuck on trying to digest my diagnosis, my very prognosis. I'm usually able to shoulder a great amount of stress...but my God...how do I cope with this? I felt like a ticking time-bomb; teetering between blowing a gasket with the result being a complete meltdown....or worse, just suffer a 'catatonically-stare-sit-and-rock-because-I-can't-deal-with-this' type of nervous breakdown. It would be one or the other...I myself just wasn't sure which one yet...let alone, which one would be the lesser of those two evils...?

Frazzled, I squeezed my eyes tight in an attempt to downgrade the squall of intense emotions churning within me, threatening to spill forth. Somewhat successful, I then glanced at the clock. It was after 2:00AM. Insomnia, a nuisance as well as the penalty for harboring such escalating anxiety...this was my sentence. Stressed, I lit another cigarette and inhaled deeply, shut my eyes again, and this time mentally willed myself to detach, just not feel. Utilizing focused visualization with rhythmic breathing (a technique I'd acquired as a Licensed Massage Therapist) I tried to evoke a false sense of tranquility while chanting...calm, have to remain calm and collected...in hopes of regaining my equilibrium; if only momentarily.

Now, doing this I can usually (key word there: usually) not only think fast on my feet but also manage seemingly tremendous amounts of stress during any given predicament (hence the reason I work so well under pressure, I guess). However, this predicament was different. This was a full-blown crisis, and I was smack dab in the center of it—but not as a nurse or caregiver. No, in this crisis, I was the goddamned patient, the frickin' victim! A roll I do not care to assume. Now, while this ability of mine to channel such intense emotions while shouldering stress does have its advantages (detaching myself enough in order to focus on what needs to be done to resolve a predicament), it also has its drawbacks.....especially if used out of context. Such as used continually on a daily basis to exclusively suppress emotion, as I had been doing over the past few weeks. I guess one could say it might be similar to a unregulated pressure cooker, with a busted safety valve. Sooner or later it wasn't going to work...and would inevitably backfire. Boom. Explode.

Now, my daughter...well, she knows my moods and also knows exactly which buttons to push to rattle me (not many people can do that, rattle me). So after my lumpectomy, her periodic bouts of concerned questioning had shifted to just plain pushing all my buttons while taking misguided stabs in the dark-- all done in attempts to get me to blow, in hopes that I would spill my guts. Amazingly, I maintained my composure. Well somewhat. busted safety valve, remember? I let her believe that (as she had decided upon) my recent bouts of moodiness—or what she'd dubbed mom's bitchiness—was somehow related to my dating life *(which throughout these past six or so years could be classified a tragic romantic comedy; a saga within itself....but that's a completely different journal)*. HA! So I had her fooled....well, somewhat. Allowing her to believe I was upset over some guy, was in a way easier. Still, she's not stupid....and sensed, and way before I'd requested that Michael and her come sit with me in the living room, after he'd returned home, that there was something major going on with me. Something of which might devastate her young carefree world once it was actually spoken of.

Leery, now almost reluctant to finally learn what that

what was, she perched on the arm of the loveseat and defiantly crossed her arms; ironically, staring me down with the same contemptuous air that I myself could propel at will. After a brief moment of me awkwardly trying to explain all of my recent doctor visits and tests, all it took was me saying, "There's just no easy way to say this guys. Mommy has...." and she was gone. She'd bolted upstairs, sobbing, "I don't want to know! Don't say it—I don't want to know!"

Mouth a mute O, I looked between my father (who'd chosen to hang out in the threshold of the kitchen for this affair) and my mother (who'd joined us in the living room herself) with a stricken *well that went swell...now what?* expression. Nudging JD off my lap, I rose to go comfort my daughter, but my mother stopped me suggesting that she be the one to speak to Ashley herself. My father tagged behind her, leaving me alone...leaving me to deal with Michael.

My parents had stayed for this exact reason, damage control. We all felt and knew that Ashley would take this the hardest. So I was relieved to have them there, welcomed their support. I would have rather had them stick around until after I told my son, but...

I turned my attention back to my son Michael, as he asked me, "Is Ashley in some type of trouble?" still unaware, and now rather confused.

Oblivious to it all, JD himself crawled back into my lap to show me an action figure, and then was off to rummage through his toy box yet again. Surveying the situation, I swallowed hard, unable to rid myself of the dull empty ache now gnawing at my soul.

"Um, no honey. Ashley is not in trouble..." I carefully began.

He now looked suspicious and asked, "So, um...is grandma gonna die or something, then?" with somewhat of a hang-dog expression.

At that I sighed, tamping down my anxiety, the anger,

as it yet again began to swell. Helpless, I glanced at JD, then back to my 13 year old as he now fidgeted on the loveseat that his sister had just fled. "No, honey. This isn't about grandma. It's about—" I hesitated.

I'd pretty much predicted Ashley's reaction. But, see, Michael...well, he's a PDD Atypical Highly Functional Autistic, and at times has a hard enough time just navigating through life's normal ups and downs. So I really did not know how he'd process this information....let alone how he'd cope. Not knowing what to say to soften the blow, I finally just told him, "Mike, I have cancer."

Looking more confused than startled, he stared at me for a brief few seconds, and then blankly asked, "Um...can I go back outside and play now?"

As the recollection of our so-called family meeting ebbed, I grumbled, "Why?" tormented, consumed with fear, anguish, and bitter resentment. Resentment, because I was being forced to face one of my life long fears. My worse fear. Not the fear of death itself, but the fear of learning that I had some incurable disease and would die, leaving my children behind. Strangely enough, I'd had this fear of mine way before becoming a parent. Just the thought of not seeing them grow into adulthood, not being there for graduations, weddings, the birth of their own children....well, the idea left such an ache in my heart I couldn't bare it. I could not bare the thought of actually leaving them—abandoning them in a sense—motherless, to fend for themselves. It wasn't right. No, it was not fair. None of this was fair!

So unable to sleep, and now once again holed up inside my office, I began doodling to pass the time, unknowingly writing: Why? WHY? WHY! as I replayed the events of the past weeks over and over trying to make sense of them. My thoughts, cluttered in chaos and became a deafening roar, shattering that false sense of tranquility I had conjured up in my mind. Why was this happening? My God, I have three children! They need their mommy! And why now? Now of all times? Dammit...I've worked so damn hard! And for what? Christ, Murphy...can't you just leave me the hell alone for once? Haven't I already proven myself enough? This is JUST NOT FAIR!

Staring at my own scribbles, I tossed my pen aside and crushed out my cigarette then stared at the items scattered about my study-desk. Three years' worth of nursing textbooks, three years' worth of notes, and both of my NCLEX review books. I almost laughed out loud. Why was I even wasting my time reviewing for the state nursing exam? It wasn't like I'd be starting that new career anytime soon. Nope, Murphy and his newest sidekick cancer had made sure of that--bastards! Instead of being a mommy, a nurse, I was now being forced to be a patient...being forced to face my worst fear...die, leaving my children motherless.

Why? I just want to know why, dammit! Is that too much to ask?

Silence mockingly pressed against my eardrums. Not receiving an answer, not knowing the reason, was just so damn infuriating. I felt stuck between that proverbial rock and hard place; with no direction, no way out, and still no answer to my simple question of why. If I could at least know why, then maybe I could better understand...better cope with this crappy handful of cards of which fate had dealt me...

"I just want to know why!" I growled, as I pulled my fingers through my hair until I tangled and balled my fist tugging in sheer frustration; as if I were actually going to pull it out at the roots. "Why me?! Why now?!"

Nothing, but sheer silence....

Exasperated, outraged, my fractured control rupture. My anger, now inflamed past the point of no return, ignited as swift and hot as a flash-fire greedily gobbling up dried timber. Enraged, I slammed my NCLEX review book shut. Not satisfied, I took both review books, along with those three years' worth of nursing notes, and vehemently hurled them out of spite. Still not satisfied an inhuman growl escaped me and, pushing up out of my chair violently sent it tumbling on its side. Surrendering to the fury, I launched an all-out attack and sent everything atop of my study-desk airborne with one efficient swipe of my forearms. Textbooks, folders, a cup of pencils, highlighters and pens, binders and note-cards, took flight and sailed across the office-- nothing was spared from my wrath.

Why?! Somebody, my God, anybody, just please tell me WHY!?!

As the last paper fluttered slowly to the floor, I stood amongst the disorder; fist still clenched....void of the gratification I'd sought from such a livid outburst. Furious, still struggling to just understand, each breath I took snagged on a bout of hiccups, which quickly escalated into ragged choked sobs. Powerless, my usual defenses incinerate, I simply sank to the floor on my knees, pleading *"Why? Why? Why?"*, then sprawled in the fetal position, a heap of shuddering helplessness, incoherently croaking in sheer agony, "Somebody just please tell me why...what did I ever do to deserve this--?" over and over as the flood gate burst, releasing the pent-up torment until there were no more tears to purge.

Spent, I then just laid there too weak to move. In the tranquil aftermath, I stared blankly at the objects of which had miraculously gone unscathed during my fit of rage. Within my direct line of vision: a collection of candid snap-shots framed and proudly displayed above and around my computer desk. Some of just my kids; others of me, Ashley, Michael, and JD together—my very own little family. Scanning those happy faces, a new grief swelled and a fresh torrent of tears sprouted to slip silently down my cheeks.

My children are just too young to be motherless...*but how do I even get myself out of this one?* became the question.

Desperately needing direction, my gaze came to rest on

a single photo. A photo of my sister and I with my grandmother—taken in 2004 before she'd passed. A strong and courageous woman, my grandmother. My mom's mother, who had possessed a feisty streak of stubbornness and sheer tenacity; a vivaciousness, which had served her well throughout her years. While alive, she had taught me many a things, my grandma. And during this, my darkest hour of utter despair and uncertainty, it was her spirited grin which leapt out from that collection of happy expressions captured for eternity. Oddly enough, as I lay there staring at that photo itself, her insightful yet rather odd words of wisdom whispered throughout my mind: *"Happy dishes do not cry in my cupboards, Deenie..."*

Now, however corny that may sound, it placated me. You see, as a child, I recalled her saying this as we were drying and putting away her dishes. Seemed logical; simple enough. Make sure you dry those dishes good. Or was it that simple? Growing into adulthood, hearing her say this same phrase now and again, I began to wonder, to suspect that maybe there was something more to it. Perhaps a hidden connotation to be left open for interpretation...maybe? A curious soul, I myself, on occasion would question her about this, among many of things...yet upon doing so, I wasn't granted an actual answer, but more of an incriminating grin with a rather conspiratorial wink.

My grandmother, she was like that. I loved that about her.

Nevertheless, when I was asked to speak at her funeral and while pondering what to even say, I found myself writing a poem dedicated to that very conviction of hers which suggested that 'happy dishes did not cry in her cupboards'. It just seemed fitting, as it had been those exact words, which had comforted me, my grief, and had allowed me to cope with her passing.

While contemplating that silly little phrase of hers now, at my darkest moment, this time...well, this time something extraordinary occurred. Something that of which had perished within me during my fit of fury now began to stir. Astonished, I slowly sat up and glanced around my disheveled office. Eyes resettling upon that photo, an absurd grin twitched and then curled my lips. I sent that spirited expression of hers a conspiratorial wink and confirmed out loud, "Nope...they don't", and then whispered, "Thanks, Grams."

Picking myself up, I dried my tear-dampened cheeks then assembled my best game-face. Marshaling the courage to stare death itself square in the eye, I lifted my chin in ultimate defiance—unwilling to accept such a fate—and then boldly snarled aloud, "Bring it on, Murphy. Give me your best shot, you bastard," in direct challenge, then added half under my breath, "...because this time, you picked the wrong bitch to mess with!"

Wielding a fiercely tenacious stubborn streak, and hope, as her only weapons—a gift passed down from my great grandmother, to my grandmother, to my mother, and then to I—the warrior within had just awoken, and was prepared for the battle of her life.

Journal Entry August 2008

I spent most this week on the phone, speaking to people of whom I didn't see on regular basis, but still considered my close friends. Somebody had to tell them, the handful of friends who lived too far away. I figured who better to tell them than me. I dreaded it…having to share this news with them. It's not something you want to tell people over the phone. It's hard enough to tell people in person. There is just not a good way to tell people you have cancer. I guess one could try to sneak it in between chitchatting about how fast the kids seem to be growing and the price of gas. Perhaps slip it in between bouts of gossip, such as, "did you hear about so and so…I know, crazy isn't it? Oh hey, guess what, I recently got dealt the death card myself. Yeah the big C. Crazy isn't it…"

The first two phone conversations were uneasy and stammered, as I had no clue really what to say let alone how to bring up the subject. By my third call, I had it down to quick and simple, no beating around the bush. I simply just told them. I first made sure to ask the person receiving the news to sit down. I realized to request that they sit down, only after a friend dropped the phone in shock once hearing the news. I did not give them all of the details, nor did I mention the seriousness, or of my grim prognosis. I simply told them I had advanced breast cancer. Stage III-B with triple negatives only if they happened to ask. Some did and knew exactly what that meant, while others had no clue. All and all, I think I did a pretty good job sugarcoating it. That twisted humor of mine helped. And for those who did not understand my twisted humor, well to stop the sobbing that always ensued my announcement, my reassurance became: "Really, I'm fine…this is just a minor bump in the road…no big deal. Everything is going to be okay." …as if saying it would actually make everything all okay.

Phase Two: Trapped within the Chrysalis

Author's note…

One of the most truly amazing occurrences of nature is complete metamorphosis: literally changing from one creature into a completely different creature…such as the caterpillar into a butterfly. When a caterpillar is fully grown, it instinctively searches out and then attaches itself onto the safest point of leaf or a twig. Once securely anchored solely by its hind claspers, it releases its hold of the twig to literally dangle upside down—vulnerable and unprotected—doing so willingly to allow nature to take its course; trusting in God's divine plan. As it pupates it molts, discarding its outgrown skin for the very last time which forms a harden shell called a chrysalis. While encased inside this seemingly lifeless and immobile vessel, it appears to the outside world there is little to no movement. Yet, secluded within total isolation, something extraordinary is underway…for it is during this time—the chrysalis stage—that growth and differentiation occurs; complete metamorphosis.

Instinctively, the warrior within had awoken…sure. And I, myself, was pretty much ready to rumble; prepared for battle…but I was fighting for the old life; the life that I liked and had grown accustomed to. I simply had no clue. So in all actuality, the real battle had not even begun yet. Of course, at this time, I did not fully appreciate nor did I even understand this. So I was unaware of what exactly this journey would entail. I was oblivious to what sacrifices would be required for such a life-altering passage.

In retrospect, all I really had to do was let nature take its course. Much like that caterpillar, I would have to adapt; accept and trust in God's divine plan; willingly surrender control, give up my outgrown skin. First, however, I had to talk myself into just letting go of the damn twig…

CHAPTER 7

We shall draw from the heart of suffering itself the means of inspiration and survival. —*Winston Churchill*

Tuesday August 12th 2008 *(the real battle begins)*

Not really knowing what to expect, I arrived at Medical Associates chemo lab bright and early to begin what would be my first phase (three months) of chemotherapy treatments. My mother—a veteran of chemotherapy—tagged along. I guess to both support and guide me through this…well, this rather unexpected and much unasked for rite of passage.

"Pick a recliner," my mother instructed then explained, "One of the girls will be with you shortly. They're all busy right now."

"Um…okay," I mumbled glancing about my new surroundings as my mother busied herself with greeting people—by name.

My mother it seemed knew everybody; or everybody knew my mother. So no matter what the circumstance or situation, wherever we happened to go she knew at least a few, if not most of the people, there. The chemo lab apparently was no different. As she socialized, I eyeballed the three rows of plump and comfy oversized LazyBoys provided. Stationed strategically around the room were several flat-screen TVs most of them set to *Good Morning America*, *CNN,* or whatever early morning news program were on. As I stood there still deciding which *LazyBoy* to claim for myself, I couldn't help but to feel extremely uncomfortable and slightly out of place. Staring at me with curious yet 'oh so young, isn't that a shame' empathetic expressions, was a roomful of older, elderly, patients. Half of which somehow or another knew my mother.

Figures. Not like this was some social function for meeting new friends or anything, but my God, at thirty-eight years young, I was the youngest patient there.

Heaving a sigh, I picked a recliner and sat; a little impatient to get this started and more than a little nervous. A nurse finally made her way over; one who I hadn't met the day of my tour. Doing the whole double take between me and my mother she shook her head and exclaimed, "Are you kidding me?" Then without missing a beat jokingly announced, "Just so you both know, there are no two for one family discounts given here."

At that I laughed. Cool, a nurse with the same twisted warped sense of humor as mine. I relaxed instantly and settled myself as she explained that she would first have to take blood from my new port, the medical device which had been surgically implanted (the day before) below my left collarbone, just underneath the skin. See, this port was basically a central line which would protect my regular veins (the ones normally used for IVs and blood draws) from the harshness of the chemo drugs themselves. This port would also allow them to give me multiple drugs simultaneously.

My cocktail this morning, and for every treatment thereafter during the next three months, would first start off with a dose of steroids; to help counteract the ill-effects of chemo drugs—or in other words: to prevent me from becoming violently ill. After that infused, it was then on to the actual chemo drugs themselves. Due to the advanced stage of my cancer, I would be receiving a combination of two chemo drugs. My oncologist referred to this combo as *"the heavy hitters"*. Cytoxan (generic name: Cyclophospamide) and Adrimycin (generic name: doxorubicin) which is actually a type of antibiotic, but like none you ever had before or will again. Interesting factoid: this rather harsh chemo drug has nicknames both because of its harshness and also its unique color—bright blood red. Some call it The Red Cure, The Red Devil and, or Hi-test Hawaiian Punch. And I was told not to be alarmed because it would make me pee bright red. Gee, lucky me....huh?

So, while a bag of Cytoxan infused, I also received a turkey-baster sized syringe of the Adriamycin. Now receiving this Adriamycin for the very first time, I was...well, a wee-bit concerned to know exactly why on the earth the nurse giving it to me was now dressed head to toe in plastic protective gear; sporting thick rubber gloves that went up to her elbows, as well as was wearing one of those full clear plastic face shields.

Seriously, she looked like a Smurf clad in this baby blue gear.

When she draped a baby blue plastic chuck across my chest—with intentions of injecting this stuff in my port—that did it, and I finally demanded, "Hey what's up?" She informed me that this drug was so potent that it was similar to acid...meaning it would literally eat your skin away and pretty much any clothing that it came into contact with. Hence, the reason for her fancy plastic baby blue attire.

I glanced down at the flimsy disposable chuck, and felt sort of jipped.

Whoa...this crap can and will eat off your skin? Okay, now wait just a damn minute! This drug is so potent—

potent to the point that you have to dress head to toe in plastic protective gear just to handle it—yet you are still planning on, let alone have no problems whatsoever, with injecting it inside of my port? In doing so pumping ME full of it? Ah...I sort of have a teeny-tiny problem with that. She explained that because my port was a central line (meaning it was plugged into a really large vein) that as the drug was infused my blood would basically dilute it and therefore I would be okay. Or at least my insides would be...

Uh-huh...sure...okay...um, sorry not buying it. I mean, yes I admit as a nurse I understood the logic...but...well, as a patient I was a tad apprehensive. I mean seriously, she was dressed like a Smurf and wanting to pump me full of some bright red corrosive flesh-eating drug that had a handful of nicknames and would make me pee bright red!

Reading my concern, she did what any good nurse does...she actually took the time to talk to me as a human. Afterward, I let her administer the stuff. At least after she completed the process of slowly injecting it via my port, she didn't readily flea...you know, like Mr. Comical had after pumping me full of his 'radioactive gunk'. In a way, I was a little relieved. Until, of course, I realized why she was sticking around. She was doing so for observation; to make sure I didn't have any adverse reactions....such as, well for starters: instant death, you know, due to heart failure...because we all know that right there can prove to be potentially fatal.

Sure, I'd read the info they had given me. I knew the risks. I guess it just hadn't occurred to me, until right then and there, that the drugs they would be pumping into me to kill the cancer growing within me, might actually kill ME in the process.

They were to all intents and purposes poisoning me in hopes of keeping me alive.

Unnerving contradiction. Yeah, I know.

So anyway, while these powerful drugs infused for the

very first time, the nurse sat beside me to both observe and to educated me on the ins and outs of chemotherapy itself. We of course went over the basic side effects: extreme fatigue, nausea and vomiting, hair loss, joint pain and unusual weakness, just for starters. What to watch for. What to do. And, of course, when to call my doctor. If need be, to call him at home no matter what the hour. Then I was given a thermometer and was told to take and keep a record of my temp on a daily basis. Then of course she explained to me that I should try and avoid crowds, small children (um hello, I'm a mommy remember?) and to avoid exposure to the general population at large...all of this to be done in order to protect myself from...well, from acquiring germs and prevent infection.

You see, chemotherapy obliterates a person's immune system, completely destroys white blood cells, therefore the body's ability to defend itself and fight everyday germs and infection basically becomes null and void. So my newest mission (I mean, besides beating this stupid cancer to pulp), during the course of my chemotherapy, was to protect myself and avoid common everyday germs. Germs, which so happen, caused all those common everyday infections. Because with a suppressed immune system, a person can become extremely sick and/or...well, under these circumstances, worst case scenario: die.

Yeah, I know, sounds impossible. How does a single mother of three kids avoid germs?

The nurse suggested that I wear a mask if/when out in public to protect myself from these germs (great...I had visions of Michael Jackson). And to have somebody take over care of my kids if/when they happen to become sick themselves. And I am not talking major infections either...I'm talking about your everyday common cold and such.

So okay...let's see. Single parent, raising three kids. One of which who was two years of age, so still somewhat a toddler, in daycare (and well we all know daycare is a breeding ground for germs). Um, question: who do you propose I find to "take care of my kids" if in the event they themselves become sick, so I can myself avoid their germs...? I didn't have the luxury of a significant other to take over, let alone take care of me and/or to help out. All I had was well, myself and my parents. And my mother, was at the time still undergoing treatments and battling cancer herself.

Overwhelmed with the idea, I did not feel like going into those very issues with the nurse, at the time, so I simply switched subjects. Knowing that most chemo patients lose their hair, I wanted to know how soon to expect that to happen. When I asked her how long it would take to lose my hair, she couldn't give me an exact answer. She could only state that it happened usually within three weeks give or take, as each person was different.

I actually hated the idea. Losing it, my hair. See, my hair—at the time, was almost to the middle of my back. And although it sounds petty and crazy, I loved my hair.

One of the nurses—after a few of them had joined in on the conversation, all sympathetically examining my long locks themselves—excused herself, then returned with a pink handkerchief. I took it and simply stared at it. Pink had never been a favorite color of mine...in all actuality I loathed the color pink. Her advice was simple yet somewhat hard to digest. In order to avoid the mess *(it's a slow progression which only gets worse, as I know this due to seeing my mother lose her own hair to chemo)*, and spare myself the mental and emotional anguish of actually losing my hair to chemo, she suggested (because my hair was so long) that I might want to consider just shaving my head.

Okay....so not only had I already agreed to give up both breasts, now I was also being asked to entertain the idea of shaving my own head...? What's wrong with these people; what was wrong with this picture? Although I did somewhat agree with and understood her concept, it was somewhat of a shocking idea. I just wasn't quite ready to race home and buzz my long beautiful hair clean off.

I thanked her for the bandanna and her advice.

During that first chemo treatment, my cousin Becky stopped in on her way to work. Growing up together, it was during our teenage years that we'd truly bonded, creating more of a sisterly link between ourselves than that of just cousins, always there for each other during times of need. And so, just by reading her expression, her body language, I could already tell this impromptu visit of hers held the potential of becoming extremely emotional.

Wonderful.

Wanting to avoid that, I greeted her poker-faced with a simple, "Hey."

Looking a tad uncomfortable, she glanced about and then commented, "So this is the chemo lab, huh? Pretty nice."

After a second of catch-up with my mother, she then got up. Offering Becky her chair, she excused herself so that we could visit. Declining it, Becky explained to both of us that she couldn't stay long. After another few excruciating seconds of playing let's-pretend-there's-nothing-wrong-here via inconsequential small talk, she then told me the reason for her visit.

She'd stopped by to visit briefly, but mainly to give me a bandana that she'd acquired a few months prior to any of us ever learning of my diagnose. Pulling it out of her purse, she explained she'd bought it from a coworker who had been selling them to raise money for a breast cancer fundraiser biker run *(later I realized this was the same exact group that I myself was invited to ride with, as a survivor. An Illinois based group called Team Underwires)*. Becky then stood there awkwardly fidgeting with the bandanna itself, not really knowing what else to say, expression troubled, eyes already brimming with tears threatening to spill forth.

"Stop it, dammit," I half hissed half croaked, and then warned, "If you cry, I cry."

Nodding, she shoved the bandanna at me then pretended to watch one of the TVs while composing herself. I took the opportunity to do the same while examining the bandanna itself. Of course it was pink. But unlike the generic bandana the nurse had earlier given me, this one was rather unique with its breast cancer ribbon symbols screen-printed all over it in bold black ink. The breast cancer ribbons themselves had a biker chain overlay, making the symbol itself a double ribbon. Printed next to each ribbon was a rather challenging enquiry: TOUGH ENOUGH TO WEAR PINK?

So, okay, I must pause to state: Number one, I seriously hate the color pink. Pink was Becky's favorite color, not mine. And number two: I for one would have never once equated the color pink with being tough. So this bandanna, with its bold cheeky question printed all over it was well, fitting. I don't know, call me strange— heck, maybe the planets and stars were all in perfect alignment?—because, in a corny sort of way it was almost as if the damn thing were asking me if I thought I was tough enough. Whether Becky picked up on that herself, I still have no clue. Maybe she had? Maybe on some unconscious level she knew that at this particular time in the time-space-continuum this stupid bandanna was just what I needed...? Or maybe, it was just me. Regardless, it was exactly what I needed and here she was now offering it to me.

"The guys, they wore them mainly," Becky said—and queerly enough, as if needing to clarify the bandanna's proclamation itself, and then rambled on, "I mean, I think anyway. I wasn't there. But the material, it's...well, it's thicker, and it's bigger than a regular bandanna. So, well, I just figured it would last longer. You know, being of better quality it shouldn't wear out as fast."

Ok, she had a valid point...so I nodded in agreement, still not really sure what to even say. I don't think I'd ever seen my cousin stammer in such a manner before.

"Um...I bought them way before you'd been—well, that's sort of weird, huh. I mean, who would of guessed that you would be—and then I would have—well, I never thought—" Clearing her throat, she looked around again. "Anyway, I just thought I'd give it to you, um, you know, to use—well, wear, um once...well, for when your..." she stopped, unable to say it.

"I'm thinking of buzzing it off," I announced to spare her having to say it.

"Oh—k...? She stared at me, visibly horrified at the idea, and then quickly recovered with, "Well then...um, well there you go. See, so you can wear it when you do."

"You sure?" I asked.

"I bought two of them. Not sure why? But yeah, it's yours. Um, if you want it."

We started at each other a long moment, both of us struggling to keep our emotions, and tears, in check.

"Thanks," I croaked then scolded, "You promised, dammit," seeing her eyes swimming with tears as she leaned over to give me a hug. After she straightened, and after another moment to compose ourselves I snorted, "You do realize I hate the color pink, right?"

"Yeah...," she half sighed half laughed, and then gave the idea itself a lopsided frown. "Go figure, huh."

A couple of days after that first chemo treatment, I decided to buzz my head. It was after 1:00AM when I decided upon doing this. On a mission I searched to locate my clippers then bravely, and without hesitation, took three swipes shaving my long beautiful hair clean off; starting right down the center of my scalp, then a swipe on either side. It was after that third swipe that I hesitated. At this same time my daughter poked her head inside of the bathroom.

I was fine, or had been, up until that point.

We stared at each other via the mirror for a split second—me holding a pair of clippers looking red-handed as if just caught doing something wrong; she gapping back and looking rather stunned—before she blurted out, "Oh my God, mom! What are you doing?"

"A G.I. Jane," I quipped, not missing a beat and as if nothing was at all wrong.

Not understanding what I had meant, she glanced between my half-bald head and the floor. Tracing her gaze, tears seared my eyes once I allowed myself to survey the mess of hair covering my feet and the bathroom floor.

"I....I," Unable to form words, I stared at myself in the mirror, as I slowly brought my hand to my buzzed scalp and touched it. That made it real. *Oh my God. Oh my God. Oh my God...what had I done?* "I...I can't see the back, um, I mean to finish it," I then managed to sputter in between choking sobs.

Some therapeutic save yourself some emotional trauma experience this turned to out to be. I still believe however that buzzing my own head was a lot better than letting chemo take it strand by strand.

Unable to contain her own dismay, my daughter's face reddened as silent tears sprouted and started rolling down her cheeks. Without another word between us she stepped inside the bathroom, shut the door, and took the clippers from me. Neither of us spoke as she shaved the rest of my long beautiful hair clean off. By the time it was all said and done we were laughing in between sobs.

About a week and a half later my stubbly G.I. Jane buzz cut completely fell out due to the effects of the harsh chemo drugs. Having had buzzed my head with my daughter's help, I thought I would be okay with it. But nothing can prepare you for handfuls of stubble. What a mess! And so yet again, I found myself morning the loss. I realized I simply wasn't at all prepared, mentally or emotionally.

My mother, the chemo veteran, took me to Davenport for a day of shopping and lunch at the Olive Garden. We then stopped at a little shop where she'd purchased her own wig and told me to pick one out. We had a blast, giggling like little girls while trying on all the various wigs just for fun before getting serious and picking one out for me. She purchased it for my upcoming birthday. A guy whom I had recently met and was somewhat dating, thought it was hot and loved it! I too liked it, but I just could not get used to actually wearing it all of the time. It was hot and itchy...and just felt strange. However beautiful the wig was, it just wasn't my real hair. So most of the time, I kept the wig on its Styrofoam head and instead simply wore my **TOUGH ENOUGH TO WEAR PINK?** skull cap.

Journal Entry September 4th, 2008

Today I am officially 39 years old and I have an extremely nasty case of oral thrush (you know the stuff that infants usually get? Yeah, that. It sucks), all thanks to chemo. My mom and dad came over tonight to celebrate my birthday. I was too sick to go anywhere, so mom ordered pizza. But for me, for my birthday, it was whatever I wanted. So she ordered lasagna from Vitales. I love Vitales' lasagna. I was so looking forward to savoring each and every mouthful…but my mouth and throat hurt so badly, I couldn't eat it. It hurt to swallow and I couldn't taste anything beyond the nasty gross stuff coating my mouth and throat. And on top of that I just felt like shit.

Happy birthday to me, I guess.

Lately, I've become so rundown due to chemo and have become extremely dependent on my oldest daughter Ashley to take care of the everyday things around house, as well as to help with her youngest sibling JD. I am becoming too weak to keep up with my two and half year old. I hate it. For a couple of days after chemo, I have to literally lock myself in my room. Not to recoup actually, but to avoid people and germs in general. For two days after chemo, when I go pee I have to flush twice. Yes you read that right…I was told to flush twice and because I had pets, I had to make sure everybody in the house remembered to shut the lid so the animals could not drink out of the toilet bowl do to the possible trace residue from the chemo drugs. Yeah crazy…

I'm usually higher than a kite for the first few days after chemo, due to the steroids they have me taking. Then after that I crash and burn and feel like I've literally been hit by a Mac truck. If I'm not nauseous, or hurling my guts, I'm popping pills so that I don't. I don't know if it's the drugs, or if it's the chemo itself but a couple of days after a treatment I become trapped in what I've dubbed a "drug induced zombie fog" because I'm totally useless.

I am finding I have become extremely forgetful. I have to make list for everyday normal tasks. I saw a T-shirt the other day online that read: "I've got chemo brain. What's your excuse?" I should have purchased it.

If it's not the chemo then it's the drugs. I'm not a big pill popper. I hate taking pills. Hell I have a hard time remembering to take my vitamins...and now I have so many different scripts for various drugs it's hard to keep track of all of them. Got a side-effect from the chemo? Here take this drug. Get side-effects from that drug? Here's another drug to take care of that...and so forth and so on. Take this for that...and that for this...nevermind you might turn purple and sprout stripes....you won't care because you'll be so snowed you'll sleep for weeks.

I'm just always so damn worn out and tired. My energy has been zapped. So I guess skipping my birthday this year is no biggy.

Oh, and I almost forgot. The guy I'd been seeing, well he changed his mind...as in he decided today that he didn't want to be serious (this after begging me to go out with him in the first place), as in have a serious relationship with me. He told me he wasn't sure he even wanted to hangout now because it cost him too much to drive up every night from Davenport. Um hello, it was never my idea for him to come see me every flippin night in the first place. Um, okay...

The kicker? He told me this via text messages. Yeah, no great loss there, right? He actually did the whole 'it's not you, it's me' speech, well via text message.

Wow really? That was a first for me. The first time I'd been dumped via a string of text messages. I have to guess he just could not handle dating somebody with cancer. I mean we met right around the same time I'd been diagnosed, so he knew. He cried when I told him. I had given him an out then. Had assured him that if he wanted to end things and not see each other, well that I'd understand. He told me no way, he wasn't like that and stick it out. And he did, amazingly he stuck around and started coming over to my house damn near every night. But that didn't last. I could be wrong, but I think the whole cancer thing was the main reason for his sudden change of heart. I mean, I'd given him the out. But he had stayed...at first. I guess shaving my head, then totally losing my hair altogether to chemo, might have had something to do with it...made it more real...?

Whatever the reason, either way, rejection bites...cancer or not. Nobody likes breaking up...especially on their birthday...

CHAPTER 8

"Resistance is futile..." —*Star Trek, The Borg Collective*

Despite chemo-treatments and what seemed like daily doctor appointments I still wanted to maintain the old lifestyle. I just wanted to have a normal life *(whatever normal is)*. Yet what was once typical everyday life wasn't mainstream anymore. Everything that I'd taken for granted, everything that I had grown accustomed to had become distorted. Everything was changing. I was changing. And what pissed me off the most? I had no control over it. Nothing was the same. My own reflection was becoming unfamiliar. My daily routine had become foreign. It was as if I had been cast off into some alien world to fend for myself alone; forced to navigate an unfamiliar landscape without the benefit of a compass let alone a roadmap.

The more I struggled and fought this process the more frustrated, and depressed, I became. Wherever I went, *it* was there. I could not escape it.

I realized this one day while shopping at Hy-Vee. I was grabbing a cart and minding my own business, when a total stranger came up beside me to divulge, "I wasn't as young as you are, but I once wore one too," in a hushed tone. Nodding at my pink skullcap she clarified, "I wore one of those. It eventually grows back. I promise."

Caught off guard, I stared at her speechless. Sizing up her short thick hair, I wanted to ask her just how long it took to grow back. I wanted to then tell her that she was probably closer to my age than what she'd thought *(for some reason people always guess me younger, by five to sometimes even ten years my age)*. I didn't though, didn't ask about the hair growing back nor did I explain the age thing to her. I simply stared at her and said nothing.

Actually, to be totally honest, I had no clue what to say.

Don't get me wrong, I do not mean to sound...well, unappreciative of a stranger's kindness. I just didn't know. Were we supposed to exchange details, share stories? Discuss and compare notes? Talk about our diagnosis? I had no clue. This was all new to me. Although she had taken the time to approach me, I was positive this woman did not have the time to answer a bunch of silly questions...so I simply said nothing at all.

What I didn't understand was how it all worked: this grand induction in to the Sisterhood. All I knew was that I had been unwillingly recruited in to this elite club—of which, I myself would have much rather totally steered clear of to begin with.

Despite the awkward lull of silence my lack of response caused, the woman offered me a warm smile. "Good luck to you. Keep your chin up and fight like a girl."

As she walked away to rejoin her two teenage daughters, I managed to mumble a meek, "Thanks," before she was completely out of earshot.

Glancing backwards she smiled and waved, then was off to do her grocery shopping. Standing there, I felt like a complete and utter moron. I felt the pang of guilt, right alongside the vague sense that I had possibly just blown some marvelous opportunity. But seriously what was I supposed to say? Do? It wasn't like this Sisterhood thing came with a rule book of protocol and etiquette. Or did it?

Was there some sort of secret handshake? Did I miss my issued membership card in the mail? Were we supposed to exchange phone numbers so that we could chitchat over coffee; perhaps do lunch?

I simply had no clue…

Since the day of my diagnosis, my mother had been nagging me to find a cancer support group. She told me I should find people to talk to. Although I had checked around town, only to discover there were none for my age group, I did not feel I needed to talk to anybody about 'it'. Already a month in to chemo therapy I figured I was doing fine. Did I really need to discuss with others the pitfalls of chemo, share stories, and talk about how much cancer sucked in general? Publically express my fears…?

What a bunch of malarkey. Besides, I didn't need to talk to bunch of strangers. And even if I wanted to, there weren't any support groups for my age group. I mean seriously, how is a 50 to 60 some year old going to relate to a 38 year old single parent dealing with cancer while raising three kids? So I simply ignored my mother's advice…until of course, her own prognosis took a nose dive.

As I had mentioned, my mother had been battling cancer herself on and off for over three years. However, this was not the first time she'd battled the "big C". She had had skin cancer, twice, when I was little…too young to really remember. The only memory I still have was of her being wheeled out to us, my sister and I, after a surgery (it might have been a day or so afterwards, not really sure?). Still, I recall a nurse wheeling her out via a wheelchair so that we could see her and know she was okay.

She gained two scars from those two separate battles. One was on her forearm and other was a huge crater where they had scooped out a hunk of flesh a few inches above her knee. As I said, I don't really remember much of the actual experience except I do recall the nightgown and robe my mom had insisted on wearing for our visit. The top was the color red with white and black, and it…well it simulated a hanker-chief type pattern. The flowing ankle length gown was dark navy blue, and looked similar to that of denim. Don't ask me why I remember this…as I have no clue. Nor do I know why she insisted on wearing it for our visit?

As an adult, I can only assume that she'd done so because she didn't want us to be frightened seeing her in the hospital wearing a regular hospital gown. At the time, I don't think I was even aware she had cancer—not until I was older anyway. See, even back then she was trying to protect us; sugarcoat the truth.

This time, however, I wasn't a child. I was an adult; had the right to know. My mom was battling an extremely rare—as well as aggressive—form of uterine cancer. Despite surgeries, multiple rounds of chemo in addition to multiple rounds of radiation, it just kept coming back…her cancer indeed was proving to be relentless. And although she was granted brief spells of remission, it just kept coming back…so, she never completely won her own battle.

I can't recall the exact day, but remember when she first mentioned to me she thought something was amiss. She kept telling me about her signs and symptoms, and I repeatedly kept telling her to go see her OBGYN. I don't think she did, not right away. When she finally did go, I think it was too late and they knew right away that it was cancer, but she wasn't telling anybody anything of the sort. She was worried, I could tell; could see it. And I sensed that something was wrong even though she played it off.

They ultimately did surgery (a radical hysterectomy; took lymph nodes, surrounding tissues and then some) she went through chemo and then radiation. At one point, I believe she had chemo and rad at the same time (although I am not certain). When all was said-and-done, she then announced the doctors' had given her a clean bill of health.

Then it struck again. More chemo, more radiation.

Then another clean bill of health. This time I had a hard time believing that....but it seemed she was doing well and so it appeared she'd beaten the big C yet again. She did well for a while, and then, like a bad penny it was back yet again. I remember the day when my mother had informed me it had returned.

When her cancer had come back, I was in college *(working toward my second career goal)* and I'd gotten a D on a major exam. I usually pulled As and Bs. Now, the nursing program within itself is stressful enough. Add being a single parent and running a household single-handedly on top of that, and then finding out my mother's cancer was back....well, it was last straw for me and I broke. Right then and there I decided I would exit out of the nursing program and graduate as an LPN. Of course when I announced this to my parents, my mother was outraged. In her view, that was not an option. My goal was to acquire my RN. She hounded me about this, relentless. I however am as stubborn as she and my mind was made-up. In argument, I explained the facts: *"College and the RN program will always be there....you, mother, may not be..."*

Side note: We all know we don't live forever. But it's a really startling awareness when you actually realize that your parents are also growing older themselves...and someday will not be around. This was that moment.

Though she still did not like the idea, she could not argue with the facts. Therefore, I simply finished up my last rotation then exited out and graduated as an LPN, in order to help take care of my mom, to be there for my parents. Strange how life works really...that I had decided to exit out and had graduated when I had...

So while I myself was still trying to deal with the idea I had cancer, along with the effect of my chemo treatments, I now had the additional stress of my mom having to go through chemo herself all over again. She of course still tried to sugarcoat everything. Her way of protecting me, I knew. She did not want me to focus on, and or worry, about her whatsoever; so she basically tried keeping me in the dark about her own progress.

It was around this time, you see, that my mother had been going through radiation in Iowa City. And it was during one of her checkups that her doctors noticed yet another tumor growing; smack dab right next to the very tumor they had been currently treating. Yeah, crazy I know. How on earth could another tumor crop up right next to the one that they were already dousing with radiation? It just did not make any sense, nor did it seem possible, let alone logical. But there it was.

It was late October when she called me to ask if I'd buzz her head. She wanted me to do so before they started her on chemo treatments again. I agreed, of course, and when she came over we first chit-chatted over coffee as usual. It was then, when the question no single parent my age should have to deal with surfaced. But this time, it was different. It was now a twofold question. You see, I guess I'd taken for granted that my mother, own parents basically, would always be around. So in way I figured that if I didn't make it, my mom would always be there to help out, possibly raise my youngest, JD, who was at the that time only two and half years of age.

Over our coffee, I asked my mother about her appointments, her treatments and her health in general. In other words, I wanted to know exactly what her doctors were saying, thinking, more importantly, what they planned on doing. I wanted to know specific details; details that my mother still wasn't readily telling me. I no longer knew exactly what the doctors were thinking, saying, only because I had been too sick from my own chemo to go with her to her Iowa City appointments. My dad didn't really understand the medical jargon and got lost within the details, so asking him about it always resulted in "go ask your mother; she's knows more about that stuff than I do". So basically, I was in the dark and did not know anything other than what she decided to share with me herself. Which I knew, I just knew, wasn't the complete truth. She was withholding information; as any mother sometime does (hell I'd done so with my own children), she was still trying to protect me, her youngest daughter, her baby...her "Peanut".

When I questioned her about this second tumor, my mother of course tried to dismiss it as no big deal. So I asked her about a surgery she'd once mentioned a while ago, a radical surgical procedure that the Iowa City doctors had at one point discussed with her as a possible option. When it was first brought up, my mother had ultimately decided against it; due to the fact that they would remove everything which would leave her with a colostomy as well as some type of urinary bladder device *(now as a nurse I know there are several options for that but was never really sure which "urinary bladder device" she'd meant, like I said she never did tell me the real details)*. Regardless, it sounded horrendous and would ultimately render her to a life in a wheelchair. This is what she'd told me; whether or not it was all correct I have no clue. In any case, this mysterious surgery would severely degrade her quality of life and that was not the way she wanted to end up living her life.

But now there was another tumor growing, despite all of their treatments. My God, they had to do something! Surgery. Cut it out and let's be done with this! Or so I thought. So I pleaded with her to at least think about, at least ask the doctors about that surgery she'd once mentioned, to at least consider it.

She told me even if she wanted to, it was no longer an option. It was now considered inoperable.

"But that means...," Horrified, I stared at her then demanded to now know the truth. She didn't say anything at all. She didn't have too. The fear pinching and twisting her once stubborn *I'm fine, there's nothing wrong* expression told me everything that I needed to know. The silent tears streaming down her face gave me the knowledge that my mother was slowly losing her own battle and that this newly proposed "experimental round of chemo" she'd been talking about, was basically a last ditch effort. Not to rid her of the cancer, but instead was being implemented in hopes of slowing the tumor's growth—in hopes of gaining time; prolonging life...

Of course she didn't explain it that way. But I knew; now understood that this was the beginning of the end. The transition in to more palliative care would in the future surely ensue. She never did admit that tidbit aloud, not until after of the fact. But, I knew; right then and there by her pained expression alone, I knew...and understood that she herself was aware of it too. But neither of us mentioned the fact or spoke of them aloud. *(For the days and month which followed, my mom still sugarcoated the truth, which was relatively easy for her do publically as she was still pretty much active and up and about as usual. She called her newest round of chemo the magical cure, basically because it was experimental chemo. She thought it would cure her, or wanted to think so...and well, I didn't have the heart to say otherwise. I figured if it helped her believe, helped her hold on that much longer, then I'd allow her to live within her own fantasy and simply smiled in agreement each time she'd tell me "this, this one is going to be cure the, Deenie".)*

So there it was. Murphy's Law strikes again—but this time, he was packing a seemingly insurmountable one-two sucker punch. Maybe I shouldn't have challenged him...? Bastard!

"What about Kevin?" My mother suddenly questioned.

I almost laughed, but sighed and told her, "He doesn't want anything to do with him," speaking of JD's biological father.

"How do you know?" she quizzed.

"Trust me, I know."

"Have you asked him? Or are you just saying that?"

I frowned at the idea. I had recently contacted him to give him the option of meeting his son; to give him the chance to possibly become a part of his life. It was an awkward event, as I myself had not spoken to him since shortly after the day JD had been born. And he had made no attempt at contact himself. So when given the option, it did not shock me in the least that he flat out declined. After all, what did I expect? After an on again off again rocky two year relationship, he'd basically pretty much walked when I'd found out that I was pregnant; had even gone as far as to claim the child wasn't his, when he himself knew he was indeed the father.

It is hard to comprehend, as a parent myself, how a human being could be so cold hearted toward their offspring; an innocent child. I mean, how does one create a life and then simply shun it? In my brain that just didn't compute….still to this day, it just doesn't compute.

Regardless, I guess a part of me (that part which sees the good in all people) wanted to believe that maybe under the circumstance (of possibly not being around in the future) this man would at least step up to the plate; become a father to JD. Mind you, I did not want anything to do with him. I did not want to get back together with him. Nor did I need or want his money, or for him to take over raising JD. I made that clear to him. I made it clear that I simply felt that every child deserved to at least meet their biological father, at some point….and due to the situation that perhaps he might agree that this would be a good time.

At least I found some peace of mind, knowing that I extended the option. I simply did what I had set out to do. I had extended to him the opportunity to meet and accept his son.

He chose not to accept it. And accepting his choice, I never contacted him again.

"Because he told me so," I replied, then without going into great detail informed her, "I stopped by his place of work." The idea left me unsettled and cued a flash of anger—anger not directed at any one person, just at the circumstance in general—which quickly subsided to hot tears as it was at this point that I had to actually voice such a god-awful question, "So if I die, and you die...then who's going to raise JD, mom?"

She glared at me, aghast that I would even voice such a dismal forecast aloud. Then, there alone in my quiet kitchen we stared at each other, knowing. And her sugarcoated 'everything is going to be fine' fairytale capsized and fractured. We hugged, clinging to each other, feeling helpless and unsure, both sobbing at the very notion that we both might not make it.

My mother shared her own fears; expressed that she hated the idea of possibly not being there to see Ashley, my oldest, graduate, get married or have babies herself; of possibly not seeing Mike or JD grow up themselves. We blubbered like babies while pondering our fates, sharing our fears, and mourned the milestones we might both possibly lose out on. Then as crazy as it sounds, we dried our eyes and tried to come up with a feasible "just in case" plan. My mom decided then that I needed to see a lawyer to create a Will.

Afterward, I then finally buzzed her head, and that's when she yet again suggested that I go to a support group. This time however she switched tactics on me by requesting that I go with her. At this point, I knew it was futile to even argue. Regardless of whether or not I wanted, or was even ready, to go to some support group was irrelevant. I was already a part of my mother's support as much as she was already a part of mine...so I of course could not decline.

CHAPTER 9

Disappointment to a noble soul is what cold water is to burning metal; it strengthens, tempers, intensifies, but never destroys it.
—*Eliza Tabor*

Do I make the arrangements?" I asked my oncologist, in regards to my reconstructive surgery.

Dr. Beckley, my surgeon, was probably the one I needed to ask, speak to about it, but I was here at the office and was just so pumped about it I wanted to know now. I was at my regular weekly appointment following chemo, and he'd mentioned the step would be my bilateral surgery. So I half expected, or rather hoped, that my oncologist would simply go get my surgeon so that we could all sit down and actually discuss it.

You see, I'd just completed my first three months of chemotherapy and was now preparing for my bilateral mastectomy—and, as odd as it may sound, getting a new pair ta-tas was, well it was my silver lining; my light at the end of the this nightmarish tunnel... For all intense purposes (aside from me not wanting to leave my kids motherless), that promise of new boobs was the thing that had kept me going; the fuel for my battle. So I was stoked at the prospect of finally ditching the old girls and gaining that promised brand new set. Excited, I explained to my oncologist what my plastic surgeon and I had decided upon, and was rambling on about the process of expanders with implants when he interrupted me with: "At this time, I'm advising against that, due to the stage and the tumor's type. I want you to do an additional phase of chemotherapy, followed by radiation, after your surgery. Therefore, I do not recommend beginning reconstruction itself during your mastectomies." In mind that his "I do not recommend" was merely a polite way of saying no way in hell will I allow you to have that done.

Befuddled I began to politely argue, "But...I thought...I mean....well, I've already gone through three months of chemotherapy, and, and, the tumors were removed and you said the PET scan—"

"The tumors were removed, yes. But the mass had already invaded the muscle. We cannot know, for certain how far spread it is, regardless of the PET scan results. They won't know for certain until after they open you up and—"

Errrr...insert the sound effect of a needle scratching across a vinyl record, here.

Wait. What—?! Won't know for certain...? Totally confused, I almost asked him if he had the correct patient, the right medical record. I stared at him horrified, and then gather up the nerve to ask, "What do you mean, you don't know? I thought the PET scan results came back unremarkable?"

He took a moment to scan my medical recorders (talk about making you feel nervous), then confirmed, "Unremarkable, yes. But...and however wonderful PET scans are, it's just not the same as opening you up. We cannot know for certain the extent—not until they've removed and examine the tissue itself."

So in other words, this whole thing was just a big crap shoot...? They still do not know? Would not know anything until after my surgery and the pathology reports came in...? I swallowed hard at the thought; at the knowledge; the very idea.

"This is advanced breast cancer. Stage three-B, with triple negatives; a very rapid moving and aggressive cancer," he just had to remind me yet again, and then went on to further explain, "Regardless of the PET scan results, we just won't know the full extent until after they perform the mastectomy. Therefore, at this time, I feel it is in your best interest to hold off on starting any of the reconstructive process itself."

"So...are we doing another PET scan, then, before my surgery? To see if the chemo has had any effect?"

"Possible. We could. But your insurance may deny it, as it really is not necessary."

Not necessary? My jaw must have been resting on the floor and my eyes had to have been saucer sized by now. "So how much more chemo will I have to have, after surgery?"

He scanned my file, as if seeking something, and not readily answering. A touch unnerved, I held my breath and simply waited for his verdict.

"At minimum, I would say at least another three months...but, again, I won't know for certain, not until after your surgery."

So there it was. They basically did not know.

I was sent home with instructions to contact Dr. Beckley's office to make arrangements for my upcoming surgery. Crushed, all hope pretty much destroyed, I went home and first bawled my eyes out at this most recent disappointment.

Journal Entry November 5th, 2008

My surgery is this Friday, Nov 7th....a bilateral mastectomy. Which, I must add, turned out to be a battle all of itself. That is, a battle with my insurance in order to get it approved. Thankfully my surgeon's office went to bat for me. You see, my insurance had only originally approved a mastectomy of the effected side. When we found out about this, both my surgeon and I were outraged and shocked. Did they not understand the extent of my diagnosis? Did they not see the logic of a bilateral for preventative measures? I mean seriously...they had already informed me that they would not cover genetic testing as they deemed it unnecessary...so why was I surprised they felt I could get by (and live) with just a regular mastectomy...?
Idiots!

After discussing options we collectively (Dr. Beckley, his head nurse and I) decided it was high-time to give my insurance a call. My surgeon's head nurse did the honors. She phoned them and promptly educated them to the extent of my cancer as well as enlightened them to my family history (the type of cancer my mother herself was currently battling), and miraculously my insurance approved not only the bilateral mastectomy, but— low-and-behold— now agreed to cover in full the cost of genetic testing (a test that cost about $4000 dollars at the time, which as I'd mentioned they originally deemed unnecessary so was not going to originally cover it at all). In addition they also preapproved...well according to my surgeon's office, pretty much anything I needed in regard to my treatment, which I was informed included a preapproved full hysterectomy, if I so chose to undergo one.

Wow...not too shabby. Kudos to my surgeon's head nurse and their office!

We collectively opted to wait on the full hysterectomy. I've decided to see what the genetic test results are. If I do have the maker, then they'll be taking everything out. If I don't have the maker then I'll hold off on having a full hysterectomy, at least for right now anyway.

So, back to the surgery at hand....a bilateral mastectomy. The left side will be a simple mastectomy and is being done for preventative measures. The right side will be a radical.

It's time for me to say goodbye to "the girls" (the girls being my breasts). A good friend of mine dubbed them that, "the girls" a while back. She had nicknamed them that because of their size (a whopping double D and them some). Ironic, for a good portion of my adult life I've hated them, complained about the size; actually dreamed about someday having a reduction.

This Friday I will now be losing them, both, completely.

I'm not sure how I feel now...? I mean, I'd agreed to a bilateral the same day I was diagnosed as it had seemed the logical thing to do. I mean, I thought I would have by now come to terms with it—losing them both. But right now I have to be honest...I'm scared, nervous, and sad. At least I have some peace with knowledge that by having both removed I most likely will not have to deal with breast cancer down the road in the left side. But still, now I am left with the not knowing. I'm scared because I was informed that they don't know how much more chemo (or radiation for that matter) I'll have to go through afterward, after the bilateral mastectomy, because they don't know exactly how far the cancer has spread in to the muscle of my chest wall...and, I'm told, they won't know until after the surgery itself.

Scary thought: not knowing....

And I guess it's hard right now, because I had been looking forward to starting reconstruction. And now I have no clue how long I'll have to wait for that.

A friend of mine suggested that I take pictures of them, my breasts. The idea is tempting, but also sort of strange within itself. When I look at myself in the mirror I find myself wondering what I'm going to look like without them...what will I look like with breasts? Another friend assured me that breasts do not make you female. I know this...as well as I also know they're just breasts. But they're my breasts dammit!

Even though it sounds vain, I can't help but to keep thinking: what the hell am I going to look like without them?! It's just going to be really strange not having "the girls"....and right now, two days before my actual surgery no less, I am now finding it hard to accept the fact that I must somehow find a way to say goodbye to them...

Journal Entries
November through December 2008

November 7th through the 9th 2008 (my hospital stay)

I was told surgery went well. Isn't that what they always tell you though when you come to? Seriously, who's going to tell you any different?

Regardless, I don't feel swell. Apparently I came to puking. I guess I puked on the anesthesiologist himself. He told me so, when he came in to visit me to see how I was doing. He was baffled that I was still sick as he told me he'd given me everything he could to stop that certain side-effect. I apologized of course and then we laughed over the fact that I'd puked on him. He was nice about it at least and funny too…and he came in every few hours, during the remainder of his shift I guess, just to see how I was doing.

Despite the fact that I am told surgery went well, I have no clue really, as all I can see is bandages…a tight corset made from wide Ace type bandages wrapped around my chest and torso. I can't really feel any pain per-say…probably due to the morphine they have me on. But still it is strange not feel anything. I would have thought having both breasts removed would have to hurt at least somewhat.

It's bizarre, I mean this entire ordeal. I pretty much went through three months of chemo alone, that is, when my mother didn't sit with me. And now this. Hardly having any visitors at all has left me with a weird sense of total isolation. Yet in some selfish 'I don't want anybody seeing me like this, so I'm glad' sort of way, it is comforting not to be bombarded with visitors…strange, yes I know.

Other than mother, the anesthesiologist, the nursing staff, and of course respiratory coming in to make sure I was doing that breathing exercise, I really haven't had any visitors. And despite the numerous text messages and phone calls I've received, right now, I just feel—for some odd reason—well, perplexingly alone… My mother stayed awhile but then joined my father at home as they are watching my three kids while I am in the hospital.

Oh, and on the bright side, I did have one visitor…an ex-boyfriend of mine. Despite the fact that we'd broken up—I'd

93

basically kicked him out after a year or so of living together, but won't go into details—we still remained somewhat of good friends. He'd been devastated when I told him I had been diagnosed with advanced breast cancer. As my surgery loomed closer, I jokingly asked him if he was going to visit me due to knowing he had huge phobia of just being in a hospital. He'd said he would, but at the time I didn't think he would actually show up. Like I said, he hated hospitals and wouldn't even visit family when they were hospitalized, so to be honest he was last person I expected to walk into my room.

I however don't really recall his visit, other than opening my eyes to see him staring down at me. Poor timing for a visit, I guess, as he came right after my surgery, so I was pretty much still out of it. My surgery had been delayed from the original time slot given to me, so the last time I'd spoken to him I had told him a totally different frame...hence the reason he'd come when he had. Regardless, I managed a weak smile and a, "Hey", but that was the extent of our conversation...at least of what I can remember anyway.

I don't really know how long he stayed...? I seriously thought I might have dreamt it, because when I awoke again he was gone. I asked the nurse, just to be certain. She confirmed that I wasn't crazy; that a nice looking gentleman with long jet black hair and a leather coat had indeed been there. According to her he had sat beside my bed holding my hand...um, until I half woke up and puked on him as well. I do recall opening my eyes and seeing him perched near the windowsill for a while...but then the next thing I recall he was gone.

I want to get online, I don't know why? I guess just for something to do; see who's online and chat with them to pass the time...? But my laptop refuses to connect to the hospital's internet server. A nurse assured me that somebody would be in to help me connect, but I haven't seen anybody as of yet to do so. I've been in and out of slumber on and off since waking up in this room. So who knows maybe somebody came in I had didn't know. Oh well... I guess I'll just shut my eyes and doze off, for lack of anything better to do...

I awoke to voices. The person, who was promised, finally came to help me connect to the hospital's internet server. Which ended up not being IT help person at all, but instead a woman I knew. A nurse who had been one of my clinical instructors. And despite the *expression of horror she wore upon seeing me, I smiled up at her. She stood there speechless, just staring at me and shaking her head no. The nurse that accompanied her gave us both a quizzical look. Because this woman was herself still speechless, I explained to my nurse that this woman had been one of my clinical instructors while I was in college getting my LPN. The tears then flowed, of course, once this woman was able to speak. I did what I always did; I reassured her everything was alright and that I was going to be fine.*

She stayed a brief while and just visited and I explained to her that I'd graduated at LPN and also assured her once I got over this hump I'd go back to acquire my RN. She then played with my laptop and made it so I could at least connect to the hospital's internet.

Thank God, because I think I could seriously go stir-crazy just lying here in this uncomfortable hospital bed...

November 11th 2008

Today I got the bandages taken off....thank god because it was like wearing a freakin corset! I still have the J-Pratt drains, however, all three of them...one on the left side, two on the right. UGH I hate them. I was told they will be pulled out tomorrow (I hope anyway as they are real pain in the ass!).

So...taking the bandages off, I really wasn't sure what to expect, at first, and needless to say at first sight it was well sort of a shock. After a minute or two of just staring at myself and ultimately shedding some tears, I then decided it really wasn't that bad. Or so I told myself. I was okay with it...could deal with this. I then requested that my mom (as she's been staying with me to help out with my three kids and the housework) to go grab the digital cam so that we could take pictures. (Oh, and yes, I'd decided to take those "before pics" the night before my surgery...I took them myself, for myself....).

We are of course still waiting for the final pathology reports, but I was told that they believe they'd now removed all of the cancer itself. During the surgery itself, I was informed that they shot me up with a dye which turns any tissue with cancer cells in it blue~ their main concern was the lymph nodes/tissue....and doing so, needless to say, they wound up removing damn near all of the lymph nodes and related tissue on the right side, from within my neck down past my armpit and into my arm.

With that being done, I was informed that I may have to deal with Lymphedema (aka: swelling) in my right arm, due to not having any lymph-nodes. Only time itself will tell....but like I told my doc before surgery: take all of them if you must, because I'd rather be alive and deal with a swollen right arm, then have to deal with this cancer crap yet again.

So...I think I am okay with everything— how I look now without breasts, or at least I think I am. Still, it is sort of strange to look down at a completely flat chest. I mean, I went from a DD and then some cup size to zip, nothing, nada. And it might sound strange, but I think I can get used to the scars...I am actually sort of proud of them as they really don't look that bad (my surgeon did a wonderful job!). Basically looking at myself—with a chest full of sutures and dangling drains—I sort of feel like a cyborg. My mother says that it should only affirm that I am indeed a warrior as I now have the battle scars to prove it. I suppose she is right in a way. I can look at my battle wounds and now say that I can pretty much handle damn near anything that bastard Murphy (aka Murphy's Law) tosses my way....

November 13th 2008

My surgeon called this morning....pathology report/results are in. According to the pathologist, I'm currently cancer free!! When I went in to read the report with Dr. Beckley's, I swear the people waiting in his reception area must have wondered what all the hoopla was about as he, his staff nurse and I cheered in triumph. Tears of joy were shed and I thanked Dr. Beckley for this great news as well as also expressed to him what an amazing surgeon he is; in turn he shook his head and corrected me by saying, "I had nothing to with this. This was all you! You are the one who is truly amazing!"

I don't know...maybe so? I don't feel any different. I'm still me...just now a cancer free me!

I keep pinching myself....it's exciting, yet in a weird way it is also sort of hard to believe that just this past July I was diagnosed with the deadliest form of breast cancer there is...had been given a 50%

chance....and then today find out I just beat the odds and kicked that nasty cancer square in the ass! I thought it'd take...well I guess, I thought that something like this would take a really long time.

I'm told it's up in the air currently, but sounds as if I will still undergo that second phase of chemo and then of course will also have to go through radiation... But I won't know for sure until I meet with my oncologist, which will be in three weeks. And even though I do not look forward to going through all of the chemo all over again, I sort of want to just to make sure it's all really gone for good! I guess it's because (even though I'm glad to have such great news right now) I am a bit leery in some ways because my mom is still battling herself and throughout these past three or so years she had herself gotten "a clean bill of health", then shortly afterwards found out they had jumped the gun because they had found more cancer, more tumors growing within her...and now, at this point, they are not sure how to treat it as nothing they do seems to be working.

Still, I can't lie...I am currently bouncing off the walls right now due to my recent path results. It is the most awesome news to hear....and I guess if somebody right now asked me: "do you believe in miracles?" I could honestly reply: "YES! You're currently looking at one."

....now, however, we just need another miracle, this time one for my mom.

December 28, 2008

So it's been over a month now since I had my bilateral mastectomy... Since then, I passed my Nursing boards about a week after my surgery. I had no other choice but to take the exam as scheduled. I was told I would lose my $200 as there were no excuses accepted, including having Advanced Breast Cancer and just having had a double mastectomy... Wow, seriously? Talk about heartless. So I took their damn exam with J-Prat drains dangling from my bandaged up body. I decided on no pain medication for that morning as I wanted to be clear minded while taking the exam itself. Not like I thought I was even going to pass it. At this point chemo had done such a number on my brain I was lucky if I could recall how to spell my name. The poor lady overseeing the exam took one look at me *and shook her head. She asked me if I was okay to take the exam. I shrugged, and told her I guess so while also mentioning something about not wanting to lose my seat or my waste my $200 bucks.*

She apologized profusely for their companies stupid policies.

I started my second phase of chemo on Dec 8th. My team of doctors decided on four treatments every three weeks, then once that is finished I have seven weeks of radiation, just for good measure to keep me cancer free. So I should be finished with everything sometime around the middle to end of April 2009 (um, I think anyway...if I'm wrong about that just blame it on "chemo brain" =P lol).

Speaking of chemo...two words now come to mind "Oh joy"...after only one treatment in this second phase, I can already say I hate the chemo drug they now have me on. I think I'd rather be boiled in hot oil....please, can I have the other two chemo drugs they had me on before my surgery? Sure that combo was hardcore, but at least I tolerated them better. Go figure.... And for some reason the Neulasta shot they give me (to help boost my white blood count) the day after my chemo treatment now sucks big time! Once again, go figure... Before, when I had that stupid during my first phase of chemo, I had no side-effects from it whatsoever. This time around, however, it literally does me in as my joints and bones scream for a couple of days afterwards. For a couple of hours I can hardly walk, it hurts so bad... That can't be normal, can it? I actually asked one of my doctors. It wasn't my main oncologist. He was on vacation at the time, so this other doctor filling in for him gives me a blank look and answers my own question with: "Hmmmm....? You still have plenty of pain meds right?"

Of course...I have scripts coming out of my wazzo. I could supply a small planet with the amount of drugs you people push. I of course did not tell him that, I simply nodded yes, and was told to keep taking them. Wonderful, just what I want to do....eat pain pills like candy for two or three days because of some stupid shot....NOT!

On the up-side, I was given the big okay to start working part-time if I wanted to. Ironically however now that I'm a nurse and can work, it seems everybody that I've interviewed with is...well, is sorta skiddish for lack of a better word, of hiring a nurse who's currently going through chemo. Which pisses me off, yet I can somewhat understand.

Chemo equals stay away from sick people. Nurse equals dealing with the sick. You don't have to be a rocket scientist to figure that one out. Oh well...so much for starting my new career right now. It's been on hold this long, what's another couple of months or so....right? I mean, I know it's probably best that I just wait until after my treatments are completely done with...but, jeesh I'm seriously beginning to go stir-crazy sitting at home doing nothing.

At least I have all the time in the world to write...that's a bonus at least.

So anyway....basically, I'm doing good or so I am told. I'm also told I'm healing wonderfully. Okay, if they say so.

I don't know... I do know this "second phase" of chemo is sucking big time. K, well that's enough for now; I'm done bitching...

Phase Three: Emergence of the butterfly...

...before this happens, the chrysalis darkens significantly. Though you may grow impatient waiting for the beautiful butterfly to emerge, you should never disturb it inside the chrysalis. Let it emerge on its own time. If you try to rush the process, its wings will not expand... —Clay Ruth, clayruth.com, The Monarch Butterfly Page

CHAPTER 10

Until you make peace with who you are, you'll never be content with what you have.   —*Doris Mortman*

Let's face it cancer is an ugly disease that can really F with your mind. Despite the fact that you are indeed a survivor, and despite the fact that you have kicked cancer square in its ass, the aftermath of it all—the mental anguish, the distorted self-image, the depression…all of it, well it can haunt you for a really long time.

The problem was, however, nobody ever mentioned this…well, not to me anyway.

So, there I was, now a boobless survivor. I wanted so badly to just go back to living a normal life, regain that old life I'd had before. But everything had already changed and this was the point I realized that life, and I, would never ever be the same. So while going through my post treatments and still awaiting the process of reconstruction, I was now forced to begin yet another journey. Trying to figure out how to live life as normally as possible, this time not as a cancer patient, but as a survivor…, turns out that can be harder than the battle of beating cancer itself. For some reason this was an extremely difficult endeavor for me as well as exceptionally depressing.

Now I must pause and first backtrack a bit in time, to better explain. Back to when I'd first met my plastic surgeon, which I think was sometime in September 2008 (if I recall correctly as I have a hard time recalling things anymore, as my brain has been Swiss-cheesed by chemo. It's called Chemo-brain, and it's real, but I'll discuss that and it's long term effects a little later).

So I was midway through my first phase of chemo, and this of course was way before undergoing my bilateral mastectomy. Because Dr. Beckley had mentioned that it may be possible to begin reconstruction itself during that bilateral mastectomy, I of course wanted to meet with the plastic surgeon, he'd referred me to, right away. So I did, and the original plan was to start reconstructive surgery at the same time I had that bilateral mastectomy. And maybe that is why in my mind it didn't bother me, at the time—to have both breasts removed. Because I was holding on to that silver lining of thinking they'd simply remove the old girls then would do whatever it was they do to give me that brand new pair of perfect perky ta-tas.

Yeah I know…if sounds too good to be true, blah blah blah. And with the way my luck had be running, I should have known better. But still, it was possible and I seriously thought I'd go into surgery and wake up with…well, at least with the start of a new set of boobs! Like I'd mentioned, that's what had kept me going; had kept my spirit up and also kept me fighting.

After introductions and a lengthy medical history, my new plastic surgeon then explained all of the different types of reconstruction options there were. I had of course researched some of them so I would at least have a clue to what he was proposing, and we discussed at length my own options. I really wanted to start this whole process as soon as possible…like I'd mention, I wanted to wake up from my bilateral mastectomy with new boobs (as I just couldn't imagine not having boobs at all). And the only way to accomplish that would be to choose the Expander Implant option.

His nurse took multiple pictures, from multiple angles, of my breasts and my torso from the waist up. I have to admit allowing someone to snap off nude pics was, well rather odd. It was comical, because for the first couple of frames I would smile; until of course the nurse alerted me to the fact that my face wasn't in the shot itself (duh, I knew that, but it's kind of automatic to smile whenever a camera is pointed at you). We both laughed at the fact. The plastic surgeon himself then came back and took several different measurements from several different angles. Afterwards, we again discussed the various options available for reconstruction, but I was pretty hell bent on the Expander Implant option. Now at this time, of course—and mind you this was all being discussed way before my oncologist himself had pulled the plug on starting any reconstruction in unison with my bilateral mastectomy—we'd made tentative plans to do the Expander Implant surgery. The process sounded relatively simple enough.

I would have to make arrangements with my surgeon in Clinton to have my surgery done in the Quad Cities. Which I already was aware of as Dr. Beckley had mentioned that himself. So the plan originally went something like this: During my bilateral mastectomy surgery, after they removed the breast tissue, a tissue expander would then be implanted and would be partially filled with saline to start the process of expansion. Afterward, they would then continue to add more saline each month, for about six months which would slowly stretch the skin and tissue. Once the desired size was achieved there would be another surgery in which the tissue expanders themselves would be swapped out with permanent implants. Then I'd have nipple reconstruction done, which would create a nipple using skin...which would then be later tattooed to add color.

I have to assume, most females would dread having a bilateral mastectomy…but after meeting my plastic surgeon I was totally stoked, because the way it all sounded I'd actually be waking up from surgery with the start of new breasts.

Yep….sounded good in theory, but as you already know, none of that happened of course. Like I earlier explained, my oncologist had had other ideas and had put a halt to my reconstructive plans. Which sort of brings me full circle…well sort of in regards to how cancer and treatment itself can seriously screw with your head.

So you can probably somewhat better understand where the mental anguish and depression began….and let me tell you, it was a downward spiral from there.

Despite my recent "cancer free" pathology report, I was condemned to an additional three months of chemotherapy to suffer through—and suffer through, I did. Once I was finally done with that hell, I then had to endure seven weeks of radiation; five days a week, Monday through Friday. It was interesting to say the least. It wasn't as bad as chemotherapy. And the staff was pretty cool and treated a person like family. When I'd finally graduated from radiation treatment, I yet again, asked about starting my reconstructive surgery…which was laughable, due to the extremely severe radiation burns I'd acquired and was currently dealing with. Yet, I asked, because I was determined to get that promised pair of perky new boobs. The rad-oncology nurse explained to me that I would most likely have to wait of course, to let my body recoup. I called Dr. Beckley's office, then my oncologist's office— impatient, and not wanting to wait for my regular scheduled appointment to ask—and was transferred to the chemo lab nurses' desk, upon which I was informed that it would probably be best to let my body recover first (which could take up to a year), before even thinking about reconstruction itself.

Everybody I asked said the same thing; wait, let your body recoup. Ever persistent, however, once my rad burns were pretty much healed I made an appointment and met with my plastic surgeon. And wouldn't you know, he told me what everybody else had been telling me all along. I would have to wait at least a minimum of six months (a year at max), in order to allow my body to heal from everything that it had just been through (chemo, surgery, more chemo, and of course we can't forget radiation) before he would go ahead with the reconstruction process.

Ugh! I just wanted to look normal; like a female and get on with my life! What was wrong with these people? Did they not understand? I looked like a freak!

While at his office, he took a peek at what he would now have to work with; frowned at the scar tissue that the rad burns had left on my right side. He then informed me that I would not be able to go through with the expander with implants procedure as we'd planned (apparently they do this expander with implants post mastectomy as well...who knew? It was the easiest form of reconstruction). But, and just my luck, the tissue damage from my recent radiation was just too extensive. The skin and tissue on my right side, he felt, would not hold up during the expansion process itself, as it was just too thin and fragile.

I could however opt to have expander with implant done on the unaffected side, and go with a Tramp-flap on the right side. He did mention however the final product might not be symmetrical, meaning there would be a major difference between the right and the left breast.

I of course did not want that! After all I had been promised a prefect set of ta-tas. So, he proposed a bilateral Tram-flap, which itself was major surgery and would use the Trans Rectus Abdominal Muscle in order to recreate both of the breasts. This is done by using a flap of harvested tissue from your abdomen and relocating it to the mastectomy wound/scar area itself. The tissue flap, also called myocutaneous flap, consists of skin, fat and muscle and although it's cut, it is still connected to its original blood supply and simply tunneled up through the abdominal cavity and pushed out through the opened mastectomy scar, situated and then sewn in place to form what is called a breast mound.

Um okay...the only problem I had with this newest proposition was the extensive stretch marks I had all over my abdomen (as most moms know having three kids can have that effect on you). They were ugly and well to me, gross. And if I agreed to this bilateral Tram-flap process those gross ugly stretch marks would then become the skin which covered the borrowed muscle of my recreated breasts. The upshot to having a Tram-flap procedure, however, I was informed was that doing so basically gave you a free tummy tuck.

Now normally, most women have enough tissue in their tummy area to create at least one new breast. I however needed two breasts. Due to my battle with cancer, I had lost a great deal of weight (which was odd because everybody else I'd met with breast cancer had themselves gained weight) and was pretty much skin and bone, so recreating both breasts via a Tram-flap would make it necessary to use implants in addition to the tummy tissue harvested, in order to help fill out the new breasts themselves.

The only question left was what size I wanted. Wow, what a question, huh? My head was swimming with just his explanation of the Tram-flap surgery itself. Now I got to decide what size I wanted? I knew I for sure I did not want to be a double D! But I could not decide whether I wanted to be a B, or a C...? Ironic, huh...

Wrapping up the appointment, he told me to think about it and get back with him. And since we'd pretty much decided on our game plan, he told me to go home and heal. I was to call his office around September or October and make another appointment to see him. At that time, and only if he felt that I was recovered enough, we would then make arrangements to begin this whole reconstruction process.

Even though I was somewhat excited at the prospect of finally getting those new boobs, I went home and sulked. I was depressed as I'd been "boobless" since November 2008. It was now already March of 2009 and now I had to wait until October...? Were they serious? That was seven months away. Ugh!

So I finally took my mother's advice and made an appointment to be fitted with prosthetics....aka: fake boobs. Following my mother's advice, I'd checked around the Quad Cities but was told I'd have to go to Cedar Rapids as it was, at that time anyway, the nearest location for acquiring such prosthetics. In a way, I had visions of my mother and I going together. Like when she'd taken me to get my first wig. We'd make a day of it; go shopping and have lunch. You know, sort of like mother and daughter shopping for that first bra. But my mother was not doing so well and ultimately stayed home. She informed me that my father would accompany me instead. I could have gone by myself, but I think my dad wanted to go, to be there for me. Of course he did not say this, he simply stated that since I was using their car for the trip, he would be going as well.

It was sort of...well, awkward in a way I guess, that my father was the one to go with me to Cedar Rapids for my appointment to be fitted with fake boobs. I drove, as I used to live in Cedar Rapids and knew the area better than he did. During the hour and a half trip, we discussed my mother's declining condition. I probed to see what information he could tell me, and got vague answers to my questions. We arrived earlier than my scheduled appointment and the place was vacated for lunch. So I suggested we go have lunch ourselves. When we finally returned, I was ushered into the back. My dad stayed out front. He had to be bored to death, sitting in the tiny reception area while I spent half the afternoon in the backroom chit-chatting, bonding and giggling with another breast cancer survivor who also happened to be a nurse herself, all while trying on prosthetics to determine which size I should go with. I knew when he was out of his element the minute I waltz up to the reception area, proudly showing off the set of prosthetics I'd chosen; all while babbling on about how lucky I was that the lady had a set of them (they usually didn't stock sets, and so I was lucky in regards to not having to wait for them to order them) that I could take with me right now.

On cloud nine, and after parading around the tiny reception area modeling my new fake boobs, I watched my dad squirm a bit and turn three shades of red, when I stopped to ask him what he thought about them.

"Yup..." Clearing his throat, he nodded and then raised his eyebrows in question. "So how much longer you gonna be?" was all that he'd said.

CHAPTER 11

*It's terribly amusing how many different climates of feeling one
can go through in a day.* —*Anne Morrow Lindbergh*

As my December journal entry mentioned, I started
looking for work way before I was done with that second
round of chemo. After all I had sat for and had taken my
NCLEX exam *(eleven days after my bilateral mastectomies surgery
no less)* and had to my surprise passed therefore was
granted the official status of being a licensed practical
nurse *(LPN)* in the state of Iowa. But, as I'd also
mentioned, nobody at that time was hiring...well, not
hiring me anyway, as I was still going through chemo. So I
instead focused on my family, my kids. After all they had
been handed a double whammy with both me and also my
mother— their grandmother, both battling cancer at the
same time..., so of course as anybody might assume this
evoked some type of turmoil.

My middle son Michael had become obsessed with
religion, death and dying...needless to say his obsessive
behaviors, mood swings and outburst became a little bit
more than I myself could handle. I was actually grateful
when my ex-husband (Michael's father) suggested that he
could stay with them (he and his wife) for a while. My

youngest son, JD who was now 3 years old, had himself been exhibiting behavioral problems at daycare and had ultimately gotten himself kicked out of preschool (not once, but twice). Seriously, what three year old child gets kicked out of daycare/preschool? Apparently mine does. Then there was my oldest, my daughter Ashley, the one I counted on to help hold our family together while I was fighting for my life…well, the strain of it all was too much for her to handle as she was failing miserably—not at taking care of the house, the cooking, the laundry or watching over her brothers—but rather failing out of high school. Her once straight A status had plummeted to Ds and Fs and she was failing the majority of her high school classes.

So you see, not only does cancer screw with a person's health and mind…, it can also cause havoc the delicate fabric of a family itself. And well, mine was about delicate as it got. I mean seriously, being a single divorced mother of three kids (Ashley from my 1st marriage, Michael from my second marriage and JD, well he was my oops how'd that happen bundle of joy), we could have been the poster-child for "this is as dysfunctional as it gets".

Once the dust of hard battle settled and I began to feel more like myself again, I could take account of the devastation that was occurring around me. Everything it seemed, family wise, had itself been on a steep and steady downward spiral. I blamed myself as I hadn't been well enough myself to see it, to realize that my little family unit was about to crash and burn. So again, shoving that ugly animal of depression aside, I rolled up my sleeves and took on this additional battle; the struggle to somehow repair, save and keep our little family unit intact.

With the help of his regular pediatrician JD was referred to Iowa City for an evaluation. After an entire day of taking his, mine, and our family's full medical history, giving JD tests and exams from speech to eyesight to hearing and then psychological, he was diagnosed with extreme ADHD with hints of possible ODC (oppositional defiant disorder). My God he was only three years old.

Discussing the options for treating ADHD, the doctor took one look at me (still bald from chemo I just happened to be wearing my "tough enough to wear pink?" skullcap) mid-sentence and exclaimed, "My Lord, you're still in treatment, survival mode, yourself!" She then quizzed me about: how on earth I did it, was still doing it?, wanted to know how I kept it all together and how on earth I didn't have a nervous breakdown in the process.

Her questions were valid. And I often wondered those same things myself. But to tell you the God honest truth….I have no clue. I just did—just handled it; did what I had to do. So I shrugged and simply explained, "I refuse to let Murphy win." When her brow furrowed in question, I clarified, "Murphy's Law."

She nodded, now understanding and commented, "You are an amazing woman."

I declined divulging that most days I didn't feel so amazing… Getting back to my son, we agreed to start JD on medication and to begin therapy for speech and behavior.

In the meanwhile, I then worked on my daughter. I met with a few of my daughter's teachers, due to her poor grades and what they had dubbed "a poor attitude". The last straw, she'd recently been suspended for fighting with another girl in the lunch room. I'd actually received an email from one teacher that stated my daughter's attitude toward school and life in general was so poor that she felt Ashley might be on drugs. To be honest it wouldn't have surprised me with the enormous amount of stress she had been under (she wasn't partaking in drugs or at least not to my knowledge). Speaking with this teacher, over the phone, I learned that my daughter had never once mentioned what our family was—let alone had been—going through, to anybody at all. Learning that not only I had been battling cancer, but also her grandmother was, quickly changed this teacher's tune. Suddenly everything was different and she would make certain that Ashley received the resources as well as the assistance she needed in order to help her get her grades back up (although she did raise a few she still ended up having to retake a few classes over).

So, you see, regaining a foot hold in life as a survivor can be just as exhausting as battling cancer itself....sometimes harder.

On top of all of this, I was also trying to rebuild somewhat of a social life and actually allowed myself to test the waters, by dipping my big toe within the dating pool—well, it was more like a near drowning in the murky cesspool of pukes and stooges. Yeah, it was that scary. And a big mistake! I mean, what the hell was I thinking? Seriously, who wanted to hang out with a bald chick with removable boobs and hair? Oh I got plenty of dates...but once they heard the word cancer, regardless of the survivor part, they ran for the hills as if I were some contagious lepor. And those who did not readily run, those who hung out for date number two and date number three, did so only under some misguided assumption that because of my current situation (that being having no hair or boobs) I'd be desperate and somehow be an easy conquest. Once they realized I wasn't, and wouldn't be, they scattered as well...just another dent in my now battle fatigued and somewhat tarnished armor. The cloud of depression only thickened, weighing me down even further after learning exactly how very shallow and crass some men really are.

My mother simply could not understand why I was trying to date in the first place. She told me I was being impractical. Others felt that I was being foolish and crazy; that I should wait. Um, wait for what exactly? For the cow to jump over the moon...? At least in that story the dish got to run away with spoon. And I still had nobody. My God, I had just battled for my life, by myself, and had won! So, tell me, what's so impractical and crazy about wanting to move on; actually live life? I was tired of hiding inside my house like a complete lepor. I was tired of always depending on myself and going through life alone. Dammit, I wanted to live. And I wanted somebody to do that with. I was ready to seek and find my very own special someone. Was that too much to ask?

I was honestly beginning to think so.

Depressed, desperate to hear somebody tell me I wasn't insane, or a freak *(one man actually said that to my face. Called me a freak while out on a dinner date after he'd found out I was a survivor and didn't have any boobs…he asked; I am honest)*, or being foolish, I actually wrote to one of those people who offer relationship advice via a column on the internet. Yeah I know: gee, that's about as valid as let's go ask the Magic Eight Ball. But hey, while holed up inside your house, hiding from the world while you await some surgery to make you normal again, a person finds things to do to occupy their time…and reading that column was pretty entertaining….so whatever helps right?

So I thought what the hell, why not? It didn't cost anything, as it was one of those send your questions or dilemma to us and maybe out of the millions of people who did so daily, you might possibly get yourself a response, type of deals. Since I got a giggle out of reading some of the dilemmas and questions—let alone her response to them, I decided to do so and filled out the form and clicked the send icon. Now I can honestly say, I didn't think I'd ever get a response. So I was shocked when I got an actual email back alerting me to the fact that she'd actually picked my question/dilemma to use within her weekly online column to respond to, which was called Red Responds.

I followed the link provided and was simply flabbergasted to see my own name and my very own dilemma right there for the whole world to see. And since this book itself is to share with you all those inner most thoughts during those ups and downs that I endured throughout my journey, it wouldn't be fair to keep this part from you. Besides, I've damn near shared everything else already....and since I still had it (yes I saved it...not sure why, but did), I figured I'd might as well share this too. Hell, if you've ever read Red's column, maybe you've already seen it. Either way this is what appeared that week in her column:

Deena in Clinton writes:

I spent a good part of 2008 battling advanced breast cancer. At the time of the diagnoses I was 38, and I was given a 50% chance to live. I'm very grateful and proud to say that I beat the odds, and today I am a survivor! I have been cancer-free since November of 2008. Of course this entire ordeal changed me - as well as my entire life (not to mention the fact that it put a major dent in my dating and social life).

Now that my life is back to normal (whatever "normal" is), I've been trying to get back into the dating scene. In doing so, however, I'm learning how extremely shallow men can be in general. I've recently gone out on a handful of dates with seemingly decent men, yet once I mention that I am breast cancer survivor they lose all interest in me - or just want to be "friends." I never hear from them again.

One man even had the gall to tell me he found it "freakish" that I had no breasts (I had a double mastectomy, but I will undergo reconstructive surgery at the end of this year). I'm a confident female, but I am beginning to struggle with this... it can be quite depressing, some days. Am I simply destined to be alone? Or will I meet a man who can accept me for who I am? Or should I just give up on trying to date altogether until after I have my surgery?

Dear Deena,

Congratulations for being victorious in your battle! It takes a strong person to beat such a vicious disease - and an even stronger one to wear the mantle "survivor." Women who haven't experienced it, and men who haven't been closely touched by it, cannot understand where you've been or how far you've come. Cancer is more than a cellular defect. You know better than most that it strengthens as well as scars.

The words "cancer" and "survivor" freak many people out. Whether it is largely ignorance, narcissism, or a simple lack of compassion, I am not sure - but many people in the dating world are searching for the strongest, healthiest mate they can find. They are looking for someone who will be willing and able to care for them in weakness, sickness, and old age - yet, they don't want to risk attaching themselves to someone that might need to be cared for, or might not live to be 100.

Most people, including men, are decent on the surface. It's when you start to look beneath that level that you will often find undesirable traits. So, while it may seem hurtful, painful, and frustrating now when your dates scatter like the wind once they hear your story, you are actually being saved time and energy whenever the riff-raff runs. These men aren't the ones who are looking for strong, healthy relationships. They are looking for some company - and some arm candy to dress up their worlds - rather than someone to live for and die with after years of the ups and downs that create successful relationships.

Anyone who is truly interested in you is going to stick around in order to really know you. The fact that you've had a double mastectomy may not be a physical turn-on at this point, but after the seeds of love are planted and growing, that is the man who will still find you beautiful, won't see a lack of breasts, and will (to your dismay) gently kiss your scars. What will matter is that he has you in his arms, and that you are okay as you are. The fact that you will have a perfect pair at the end of the year is a bonus - not a necessity.

You aren't destined to go through life alone, and there is no reason for you not to continue to date. Not everyone is going to accept you as you are, and that's okay. The guys who run now are of the same breed who stray later on in life, or bail out when things get tough. Not exactly the kind of love you are looking for, or deserve. They are the ones who are weak and the flawed - not you. Your struggles and survival have taught you much, so don't lose the lessons just because men can be afraid and shallow. Be grateful that they are saving you time by showing you their weaknesses up-front.

As for the idiot who said he finds it "freakish" that you have no breasts, he is entitled to his shallow opinion. But, if you ever encounter another like him, smile warmly and point out that sacrificing your boobs was a challenge you met with bravery, and you were rewarded with the blessings of renewed health and a second chance at life, which means that you have been validated and possibly touched by the gods. Miracles happen every day, but they just don't happen for everyone.

Your dating struggles aren't over, but you will find your mate. While he certainly will appreciate how you look, he will fall in love with you for who you are. While he will be sympathetic to all you've endured, he will be more impressed by how you've overcome these challenges, and remained as sweet as you are. You've got a good life ahead of you, Deena. You are way too strong to surrender or conform to perception now. Just keep doing what you are doing, and I promise you that it will all click into place. Stay strong!

Red

Wow…huh? In all honesty I was touched by her sincere response. Hell, I seriously didn't expect an actual reply at all, let alone rational guidance. And that is exactly what she gave me…no hokie-pokie babble, just heartfelt advice. Somewhat the same things my mother had told me, although she wasn't as…well, as sincere about it *(I loved my mother dearly, but she could be a tad critical and controlling at times)*. So I guess sometimes advice just sounds better when hearing it from an outsider. Either way, getting that advice renewed my hope and also somewhat lifted the weighty depression which had begun to threaten my very spirit. Since my chemo was almost done, and attempting to date had proved to be a complete flop, for the time being I decided to put my energy into launching my new career as a nurse. I once again began filling out applications and sending off resumes.

Sometime in February, my persistent efforts paid off. I received a call back for an LPN position that I'd applied to at a facility in the Quad Cities. I was thrilled to not only receive an actual phone interview, but was then elated to be requested to come in for face-to-face interview. I was offered the position! While the pay and benefits were decent, of course, it was only a PRN position (which meant I would only work as needed filling in basically for call-offs and/or vacations), but that was perfect for me at the time because I was now beginning my seven weeks of radiation treatments so needed a flexible schedule.

I of course had to go through training, which happened to be full time Monday through Friday. Since I was hired to be PRN, I would have to train on every shift. I was to start my training on day shift, which meant I would be working the next two weeks from six in the morning until two in the afternoon. I would then train on second shift for another couple of weeks and then would have some training (only a couple of days) on night shift. Afterward, I would be placed in the regular PRN pool and would wait until they called me and I would of course have to work at least one eight hour shift within a six week period to keep my employment.

I loved working. Just being around other people and doing what I'd gone to college for, it just helped to make life seem more normal again. By the time my training was over, I was offered a more part time position. I however had acquired such terrible radiation burns I declined the position and was glad that I was only PRN.

During this interlude of healing from radiation and everything that had come before that, all while waiting to begin my reconstructive surgeries, all while trying to reclaim somewhat of a normal life, I began to accompany my mother to Iowa City for her own appointments. She'd been undergoing another round chemo, and was at this point too weak to drive herself (though nobody was stupid enough to say that to her aloud as she was still feisty as ever and despite her declining health still withheld and kept that I'm fine don't worry about me front of hers going). So, as I'd long ago promised I helped out. I'd go with them both when I could, and then would also drive her myself when dad couldn't take her himself.

My mother and I have always been close....but supporting each other as we battled together, that in itself brought us that much more closer. I enjoyed the time we got to share with each other. I savored our long discussions over whatever topic we chose during our drives to and from Iowa City. Relished those moments that we giggled like teenagers and the times we decided to go grab a coffee and then take the long way around, just to wander the vast U of I hospital halls to look at the displayed art work. Just being able to be there for her, as she had been there for me so many times...just to be able to sit by her side, holding her hand while watching her sleep during one of her chemo treatments....all of it, well, I knew I was truly blessed for the time I got to have with her.

In May of 2009 those visits to Iowa City stopped.

I'd received a phone call in the afternoon. It was my mom's cell. I knew they had gone to an appointment in Iowa City. I was worried because they'd been gone all day and I hadn't heard from them. I myself had not accompanied them that day due to having had just started a new position as an LPN with Mercy Living Center North. It didn't pay as much, and it was strictly second shift (3pm to 11pm) but it was in town and was also part time. And since part time paid way more than just PRN (no hours at all), I'd taken the position without question. So needless to say my tagging along to those Iowa City appointments had pretty much come to an end.

When I answered, I knew right away that something was terribly wrong. My mother sounded as she had been sobbing, and the connection was awful. Due to that, or maybe it was not knowing how to tell me, not having any way to sugarcoat it, she simply blurted out, "They've stopped chemo. There is nothing more they can do. I've been placed on Hospice. They've given me three to six months to live. I have to go now. I love you. Your father and I will be home soon," and then she was gone; she had either hung up on purpose—to shelve what she knew would be a million questions from me, or we had indeed lost our connection.

Blindsided by the news itself I stood there cell phone still pressed to my ear and chose to believe the latter.

CHAPTER 12

And the day came when the risk [it took] to remain tight in the bud was more painful than the risk it took to blossom.

—*Anais Nin*

Somehow I managed to begin muddling through this thing they call survivorship. What helped considerably was that I once again felt as if I had purpose as I'd settled into my new part time job as a nurse and I loved it. I enjoyed taking care of my residents; liked my coworkers even. Simply liked going in to work and having a daily routine again—a routine that did not include treatments of chemo or radiation or weekly check-ups. It gave me a sense normalcy once again. And when I wasn't working or being a mom, I went out with friends and had some fun (strictly girl's night outs when we'd go, as I'd pretty much given up on men all together).

So I was starting to enjoy life more and more. I do have to admit however, as the days passed it was odd not to have appointments every day or weekly, anymore. I think it dropped down to once a month which was strange. You see while going through treatments, you sort of get used to all the doctors and nurses; basically they become a part of your life, a sort of adopted family. And so, when you are told you don't have to do that well it leaves you feeling somehow abandoned at first, with a sense of not exactly knowing what to do, or what to expect. But it passes...that feeling of abandonment. The nurses and doctors who followed you through the journey, however, you never forget them as they always stay dear in your heart.

As the days grew into months, the entire ordeal itself...well, in a way it began to become a thing of the past. Even though it had only been nine or so months since getting that cancer free report card, the whole nightmare seemed like....well, it felt like it had all happened eons ago. The scars, however...the scars were there and always would be. Smooth shiny red-pink slashes stretched diagonally across the area where my girls had once been. They were real and there was no way of escaping when I saw them. Some days I saw them as ugly awful things, remnants of a nightmare I'd finally awoken from. Other days I was okay with it. Sometimes, I enjoyed the fact I didn't have to wear a bra, that I could sleep on my tummy in comfort and my back didn't hurt from lugging around such big breasts. So there were upshots. But still, I struggled with self-image. My mother as well as a close friend of mine told me I shouldn't see it as being ugly. I should view it as being a great Warrior, and my scars were proof of the significant battle which was both well fought and won.

Easier said than done. I tried to view it that way; at least publically that is what I'd tell people. And sometimes I even believe it myself. Yet still, some days I couldn't even look upon myself in the mirror when nude.

Regardless of how it made me feel, as time passed all of it just seemed so surreal.

By the end of summer, 2009, it was somewhat hard to believe that I'd spent a good part of 2008 fighting for my life. September was nearing and that meant I'd be turning the big 4...0...forty years of age. Wow. While most people dreaded hitting that milestone, for me it was going to be grand celebration. For me, it would not be just another birthday, but rather more of a celebration of life itself.

And my hair, well my hair was actually starting to make some actual progress. When I had first started my new job at Mercy, back in May, it had grown in enough that I no longer wore the skullcap or the wigs. It was still extremely short of course, but with a little gel and hairspray I was able to spike it. I'd also dyed it. The color worked with my new attitude. It wasn't what I had first expected, as it came out a sassy shade of mahogany brownish-red. But needless to say it fit so I didn't change it. It actually gave me a boost and I was back to being as feisty as ever and was simply enjoying life. And by September, my hair was of course a few inches longer allowing me to actually use a curling iron on it.

In addition, the time was now getting closer that I would be able to make that so looked forward to appointment with my plastic surgeon, in order to begin the whole reconstructive process itself. It would soon be time for me to finally get those new boobs.

So I can honestly say for the most part things were beginning to look up, and despite the inner struggle I had accepting those scars, that annoying veil of suffocating depression had lifted.

Well, somewhat, as I was still trying to cope with my mother having been placed on hospice. Shortly after her phone call, the arrangements were made and the RN who would be managing her case set up an appointment to meet with my parents. My mother requested that I be there (I would have been there for her, for both of my parents, regardless), so I had gone over to their house for the meeting. The appointment entailed a wide variety of issues, an extensive history, placing my mother on DNR *(Do-Not-Resuscitate)* status, a head to toe assessment, discussing what hospice was, what services they could provide for her as well as what they could do for her and our family as a whole.

I think my mom wanted me there both support and because working in a skilled care and long-term care facility I was myself somewhat familiar with the protocol of hospice. We ourselves had a handful of hospice patients and so I had already met and somewhat worked with the RN who was managing my mother's case, as well as was familiar with a few of the other hospice nurses as they frequented the long term care facility I worked at.

I assured my mother she was in good hands, but told her I would still be there for her. Funny, I can still see her within my mind's-eye the day we first met with her hospice RN. She was sitting there on the couch, dressed fashionably with her makeup done, wig on and combed just so, her lipstick perfect, earrings dangling from her lobes, rings of jewels adorning her fingers, bangles upon her wrist. By the brave smile alone, you would not have ever guessed that she had been referred to hospice.

The visit was extremely emotional as my mom still somewhat clung to that "every things going to be fine," mindset. There were a few times the nurse and I exchange glances due to my mother's replies to some of her questions. When asked about end of life comfort measures, my mom scoffed and point blank told the nurse, "I feel fine. Is it necessary to discuss such things right now?" I can't recall my mother's exact response when the issue of needing to sign a DNR came about. But it wasn't pretty. It was frustrating to say the least. I was glad I had gone to help explain to my mother that these things needed to be discussed while she still felt fine so that she could clear-minded choices and have peace of mind. Yet still, my mother just wasn't ready to accept it and make such choices and made it clear just by reaction alone that for the time being she felt most comfortable simply talking about pain management and what services hospice could provide for her. So that is what we discussed at length. The hospice nurse was accommodating and didn't push subjects which made my mother uncomfortable, she simply switched gears and talked about other things, which gave me peace of mind as I could tell this hospice nurse was experienced and knew exactly what she was doing and how to handle the delicate situation of discussing one's impeding death.

For those first couple of months of hospice my mother remained outwardly optimistic. I stopped by to visit regularly—and although I could see that she was progressively losing more weight and was growing weaker and weaker—during those first few months she remained headstrong, was still somewhat up and about around the house and was able to control the pain enough to function independently. She was a true Warrior. She would make comments that she didn't understand why hospice kept badgering her about what "comfort measures" she wanted, as she insisted she felt fine and couldn't understand what the big deal was? At one point, while I was at work, my mother's own case manager (as I'd mentioned we had hospice at our facility so it wasn't unusual to see them now and then) pulled me aside to tell me she'd be visiting my mother soon again and inquired about if I'd be there. As she explained why, I agreed as I was myself beginning to grow frustrated over my mother's avoidance of discussing any actual end of life plans. So we decided a "family meeting" was in order to tackle the issue together— my mother's unwillingness to discuss and make choices for that moment she would need actual end of life care measures.

She gave me the date and time that she would be visiting my mother again and I showed up as we'd planned...just in case she needed back up. My mother must have sensed something, because when I arrived she mentioned that she was expecting her hospice case manager, so I'd have to keep my visit short. Right about that same time, she knocked on the door. Yes, we ambushed her...I admit it, alright. And if it sounds horrible for us to do so…well, it wasn't really, because if you knew mother well or at all, you would understand why we had to do it. She was headstrong and stubborn. And it helped that I was there, once the hospice nurse brought up the subject. At first my mother scoffed and muttered something about not being on her death bed yet and not understanding why we had to talk about such things; again tried to avoid the topic. That's where I came in. Trying to hold my frustration, I shot back gently—yet with that same tenacity that I'd inherited from her—point blank, "Mother, please, we need to discuss this. You need to make these choices. How am I, or dad, supposed to know what you want if you don't decide right now? When you are too sick to speak, how are we to know what your wishes are? Are we supposed to guess? If you get really sick, are we supposed to take you to the hospital? Or do you wish to stay here and have twenty four hour care at home? How about I just take you to work with me, toss you in a room, and take care of you there? We need to talk about these things right now, while you're still of sound mind to make these choices, so that way we know exactly what you want us to do when it gets bad."

And that right there was pretty much all it took. My mother finally caved in and we explored the options and she finally made choices in regards to her end of life care. This all of course was done between brief bouts of tearshed and stints of laughter when my mother joked that maybe I should just take her to work with me. That became the running joke between us…me taking her to work and just tossing her in some back room if she got bad.

After that was when she got busy. I can't recall the exact date when I'd stopped by as usual and while visiting with her I realized she'd accepted her looming death and was at peace with it…or at least I had to assume this, the day she proudly read to me the obituary she had composed herself. Needless to say it was a bit of a shock. It just sounded odd for her to be sitting there sounding so pleased while reading such a thing aloud. When I just sat there, probably with a look of horror on my face while staring back at her, she then explained that she was taking care of everything; that way it would be exactly the way she wanted it and now wanted to know what I thought about it all; if I thought it all sounded okay.

I guess it was now my turn to be caught off guard. She probably realized this, and we shared a few tears when she told me by doing so—by her making all of her final preparations herself—we ourselves would not be burdened with the details during such a mournful time. It would all be done for us and we'd simply just have to follow the instructions she'd pre-prepared. She literally had a list of what we needed to do. Which, when I thought about it didn't surprise me, as that was my mother. You see, she did this sort of thing whenever she and my father would go on vacation; leave instructions with notes to where everything was regarding wills, legal papers and such, who to contact and basically what to do in case something happened (my sister and I would simply shake our heads and laugh, nod and say okay have fun on vacation). Reminding her of how she used to do that, she told me: well then this isn't much different now is it…which actually eased my mind. She was right and I thanked her for doing so, for doing all this for us ahead of time, as I was relieved actually, because in all honesty I would have no clue what to do when the time actually came.

She kept at it, as the next time I'd stop by, she asked me to go look at the outfits she'd had dad set out across the bed. She was trying to decide which to wear and wanted my opinion. Then she explained, she'd been talking to the funeral home and taking care of picking out a casket for herself; had chosen what music she wanted to be played at her funeral, and had also made up a list of people she felt would be good candidates as Paul bearers and was at the moment in the process of contacting them to ask them to do so (among all the other stuff you do to prepared for such an event). I think she had even herself typed up (and stuck on the fridge via a magnet) the long list of people (besides relatives) who she wished to be contacted when she passed.

I was somewhat floored. But I could tell this gave her peace of mind, and in a really odd way to say the least, it was probably something she could do to keep control of things and also her mind from wandering on what was to come. It did keep her busy and productive. And seeing her so positive about it all, and most importantly happy, I couldn't argue or question it. And in a way, I guess it help me to accept the fact that my mother's time here on earth was indeed nearing an end.

Her health began to decline drastically in late October. I saw this and actually debated whether or not to put off starting my reconstructive phase; told her that I could delay it a little while longer so that I could be there for her. It wouldn't be a problem. But she would not hear of such a thing. She argued that I'd already made arrangements at my place of work to take the required time off (so why switch it?); reminded me that I'd sacrificed my goal of acquiring my RN due to her health (I reminded her I could always return to college and get my RN). Still, despite her failing health, she made me promise I would go ahead with my reconstruction phase, as she knew how much it meant to me and how long I'd already waited for the actual process to begin….she told me to focus on me, and not her so much; instructed me to keep her up-to-date as she could not accompany me to my appointments as she'd once had.

So, honoring her wishes, I went ahead with my plans for reconstruction as scheduled.

CAHPTER 13

"Does it hurt?" asked the Rabbit.
"Sometimes," said the Skin Horse, for he was always truthful. When you are Real you don't mind being hurt."
"Does it happen all at once, like being wound up," he asked, "or bit by bit?"
"It doesn't happen all at once," said the Skin Horse. "You become. It takes a long time. That's why it doesn't happen often to people who break easily, or have sharp edges, or who have to be carefully kept. Generally, by the time you are Real, most of your hair has been loved off, and your eyes drop out and you get loose in your joints and very shabby. But these things don't matter at all, because once you are Real you can't be ugly, except to people who don't understand..." ~ *"The Velveteen Rabbit" by Margery Williams*

Whether it's bit by bit, or all at once....it's bound to hurt; to somewhat be painful both mentally as well as physically. I should have recognized this; should have known that borrowing, rearranging, redesigning and reassigning muscle and tissue (otherwise known as the extensive process of reconstructive surgery itself), would cue the body to go into a tailspin. That the muscles themselves would more than likely become slightly

128

confused, therefore logically pain is sure to ensue. I mean, think about it...really think about: splicing, dicing, and relocating, in order to reassign a muscle's function is bound to cause some type of internal chaos and perplexity.

I just didn't know exactly what level of chaos and perplexity I was actually getting myself in to, not until after the fact.

When I'd met with my plastic surgeon (sometime in late September or early October), we'd gone over all of the options again just for good measure, and had this time set the plan in motion: Tram-flap with implants to be done in a two part sequence was scheduled with the follow up procedures of nipple reconstruction and then tattooing to be done sometime afterward. The first surgery was done the second week of November and was a procedure to prepare my body for the "big one", my Tram-flap surgery, the grand transformation. It entailed my plastic surgeon making an incision from hip to hip to "groom the area" by rerouting the blood supply in order to "super charge" the tissues of which would be harvested and used during the second surgery.

A week or so before my first surgery, my dad asked if my new friend would be able to drive me. Wait, sorry, let me pause...as I'm sure you are probably right now re-reading that last sentence, if not scratching your head as well, thinking: Huh? Did I just miss something?

So let me backtrack a month or so in time. Back to mid-September; September 19th 2009 to be exact I'd met the man who is today my fiancé. A friend had introduced us. This of course all took place while a group of us were out and about; one of those "girls night out" deals no men allowed, as we were celebrating one my friends birthdays (I think it was a birthday anyway). For the first few days, maybe weeks (can't remember now), I didn't say a word to him about being a survivor or even having had cancer. Although I didn't hide the fact either, meaning I didn't hide the displayed photo of me (obviously sick wearing that pink skullcap) and of my mom, which had been taken at a benefit held for me in 2008; nor did I hide any of the pink ribbon breast cancer knickknacks which adorned my house (if he noticed any of it, he didn't make it obvious he knew, nor did he ask me about it).

It actually seemed he was interested in me, because after the first night we'd been introduced, he called me the next morning asking when he could see me. He then began calling and texting me a daily basis and he kept asking me out. I wasn't sure what to do with him. Don't get me wrong, I liked him, I just wasn't used to this level of attention. Well, of course, one date turned into two, then three, then four, and as we began spending more and more time together, I knew I had to tell him. After all, I would be undergoing that reconstructive phase so I needed to tell him something. When I finally explained everything, to my surprise, he already knew all about me having had cancer and being a survivor—more importantly, he was okay with it. He thought it was outstanding that I was a survivor, and didn't mind that I currently had no breasts, and well basically just liked me for who I was as a person.

By October, he was always around and had bumped into my dad a handful of times by now. So in part, this was why my father was now asking me if my new friend might drive me down the Quad Cities for my surgery. He was supposed to, my dad that is, but with mom getting weaker by the day he didn't know if she'd be able to make the trip. My mother had news for him however, and dad wound up driving her down to the hospital so that she could be there for me—her Peanut—during my first surgery. Shortly after (I am no longer certain of the actual date) my mother's strength once again took a nose dive. After falling several times due to weakness, hospice provided a hospital bed for her, of which they stationed in the living room of my parent's house.

I wasn't able to visit my mother, as I had been, due to being at home in bed myself recovering. My Tram-flap was scheduled for the first week of December and I needed to reserve my strength for that as it was an extensive surgical procedure. After a week of lying in bed, and although I still had staples spanning across my midsection and was in some pain, I forced myself to get up and move about. My mother was dying and I had decided that we would have a traditional Thanksgiving as a family. My dad cooked the turkey (first time for everything and it wasn't that bad), all the while my mother giving him instruction on how to do so from her hospital bed stationed in their living room. I prepared the rest of our feast and brought it to their house *(it was the last holiday that I shared with my mother)*.

When it came time for what my mom referred to as "the big transformation", my Tram-flap surgery, I visited my mother the day before it. In tears, she apologized to me for not being able to be there at the hospital; confessed that she was mad at this entire situation because she so wanted to be there for her Peanut (that was my childhood nickname which she still used on occasion). She kept talking about what an extensive surgery it would be for me to undergo and was so worried something might go wrong if she wasn't there. I smiled, squeezed her hand and then kissed her cheek. Resting my forehead upon hers as we always did now, I whispered to her not to worry so much about me; because like her, I too was a Warrior.

After the second surgery and once I got discharged and sent home I was again unable to visit my mom. My sister had flown in to stay with my parents, to be with our mom, for about a week during this time. I myself was confined to my own bed, in a heavy duty pain killer induced fog due to the excruciating pain I was in. When I had to get up I could barely stand upright due the nature of the surgery itself...so I was pretty much useless.

Since I could not be there myself while recovering, I called every day to speak to my mother when she was able, as well as to get a report from my father. My sister had already returned home to Pennsylvania. Mom was quickly deteriorating, yet she was holding on for reasons we could not figure out. When my dad called to tell me that she kept asking for me, her Peanut, her baby girl, it was all I needed to hear. Pulling myself together, Jim drove me over so I could be with her. By this time, two of my mother's close friends were there and had been taking turns staying at the house in order to provide twenty-four hour care for my mother as well as to help my father out.

Once there my mother took one look at me and smiled, nodded in approval and then half pointed at my newly acquired chest and said, "Woo-hoo, they look nice, Deenie." We visited as much as she could as she was having a hard time forming words due to being so weak. When she spoke, it made its way out via a short choppy hoarse whisper, which I could tell was frustrating to her. Tears already slipping down my cheeks, I told her it was okay we could just sit and share this time together. She shook her head and forced herself to speak, as she wanted to know if I was done—meaning was I done with the major part of the reconstructive phase. I reported the major surgeries were done (which really wasn't a lie as I had no clue at that time that I'd need multiple surgeries in the future due to complications), and that I felt great and was recovering fine.

She smiled up at me, tears welling in her own eyes as she whispered, "Don't cry, Peanut...please don't cry," and then straining to speak clearly announced, "You won, Deenie, we did it, you won. That's the important part, that you won." She paused to clear her throat and gather strength to continued, "And, now that I know you'll be okay, my mission here is done."

This entire time I thought I had accepted the fact; thought I had prepared myself for this. Nothing can prepare you for the death of a loved one. Knowing she was so close to death, I realized I didn't want to let go of her ever. An emotional wreck, I rested my forehead upon hers and pleaded gently, "No don't say that, mom. Don't give up, yet. We'll find you a miracle too. I promise. I'll—"

"No—" She closed her eyes, exhausted and so frail, then sighed, "—no, no, honey…mine's already been used."

Confused, I lifted my face slightly so that I could look into her eyes as she explained, "You needed it more than I did, Peanut."

When I began to argue she shook her head, and then further enlightened, "My grandbabies still need their mommy; you have great things ahead of you; important things to do and finish. I've battled long enough, I'm tired…so I told Him to give it to you, just to make certain. And it worked, Deenie…you won!"

Heartbroken, hot tears streamed down my face. I was speechless. It did not occur to me until that very moment that my mother might have sacrificed her own battle to help me win mine; that she had, as she proclaimed given up her own miracle, in order to make certain that I—her Peanut, her baby, her youngest daughter—would survive. She had always been there for me. Regardless of her own health, she had always been there; had shared her hope, her courage and her strength whenever mine faltered…and then in her last days she had hung on long enough to make certain that I made it through my surgeries, stayed to make sure I would be okay.

It was shortly after that visit—satisfied that I, her Peanut, was indeed safe—that she allowed herself to succumb to the void of pre-death unconsciousness. Shortly afterward, on December 15th 2009, on a crisp sunny winter morning, my mother finally earned her wings….a true angel among angels. To this day, I still miss her tremendously…yet I know she is up there looking down on us, always watching over me.

CHAPTER 14

We must embrace pain and burn it as fuel for our journey.
—Kenji Miyazawa

For the majority of 2010, I found myself in and out of the hospital, having to undergo multiple surgeries due to complications. Some of these were minor: surgery to correct delayed healing along the suture sites; surgery to re-lift the left side in order to correct an unexpected one and a half inch drop which left my newly recreated breasts lopsided; as well as the actual surgery for nipple construction itself *(which wasn't a complication, unless of course you factor in the fact that afterward the left side crusted over in to a big scab and then completely fell off because it didn't "take"...now that's mind-blowing right there!).*

And some were more extensive and major—emergency surgery to remove the right side implant, due to weakened tissue integrity (the implant itself was literally beginning to push out through a tiny hole created from the pressure of the implant itself within my fragile skin), all due to the scar tissue I had gained from the radiation damage itself. Because the radiation scarring was so extensive and due the fact that I now also needed my right (reconstructed) breast repaired (and another implant was pretty much out of the question), my plastic surgeon utilized a procedure called a Latissimus Dorsi Flap *(Lat-flap for short)*.

This extensive surgical procedure would allowed my surgeon to do two things with the harvest tissue—a diamond shape section of muscle and skin. The skin itself would be used to replace the area of scar tissue which needed to be removed and the muscle would take the place of the previously removed implant.

Because I'd had "delayed healing" after the Tram-flap (meaning some areas of the suture line just would not heal) I, spent time stuck inside a clear plastic tube that's called a Hyperbaric Chamber. This was supposed to help speed up healing of all the suture sites and hopefully avoid any more delayed healing. I was to do a month's worth of sessions…but after about my third of fourth session of actually undergoing hyperbaric oxygen therapy, I come down with a terrible sinus and head-cold and was so stuffed up my ears could not take it. Even after the sinus cold cleared up, I was having difficulty "diving down" as they called it and they had to stop the treatments. When they suggested that I let them place tubes in my ears—so that my eardrums wouldn't rupture during treatments, which would be yet another minor surgery—all so that I could continue with hyperbaric therapy, I told them: NO WAY, forget it!

Then, in 2011, I had to undergo yet another major surgery all due to a….well, what they dubbed a type of hernia (acquired from picking up my little one) all because I no longer had the muscles that one normally does in their abdomen, as you recall they had spliced those muscles and had used them to recreate my new breasts. Once repaired, I did okay for a few months, but then found myself under the knife yet again—another emergency type of surgery—all because my body had basically rejected the mesh patch which they had used. So needless to say it had to come out. There is still a small fragment of mesh within me, which on occasion causes havoc if it gets disturbed. I've had CT's with contrast dye to confirm it's there and they've talked about doing surgery to remove it….but local doctors, I think, are scared to cut into me due to all of the reconstructive surgery I've had (my inside are all switched around basically so aren't normal)…and I've been told despite the CT results actually locating said piece of tiny mesh could end up being a three hour fishing expedition. And I myself do not really feel like participating in such an event. So, since I have a roadmap of scars already, and since I really don't feel like undergoing anymore surgery—if I don't necessarily have to…as long as it doesn't cause major problems, that tiny piece of mesh (for the time being) will just stay put. I was recently told if continues to cause problems then it will be coming out. I'm keeping my fingers crossed it doesn't.

So the aftermath of these surgeries? Well, for starters, I can't really lift; or I should say I am not supposed to. Oh and I also now have somewhat limited range of motion in my right arm (due to the Lat-flap procedure itself the doc told me I would no longer be able to do a "rowing motion" and movements of that sort). I also cannot do sit-ups (yeah, no joke…my plastic surgeon informed me that due to my Tram-flap surgery I would no longer be able to do sit-ups, literally….um, okay, and this would be a problem, why?). Well it's a problem because the muscles that allow you to do sit-ups are also the same muscles that assist you in getting up from a supine position (laying on your back), and also assist you in sitting up if you happen to recline backward in a chair. Those muscles do a lot of important things, all of which I now struggle with. I was told I would have to literally roll over on my side and then use my arms in order to push myself up to a seated position if I lay down on my back. Before I mastered the art of getting myself up by other means, I got stuck a lot. And during those early recovery days, when it took me forever to just roll over to my side in order to push myself up, my fiancé helped by rigging up a thick rope to the underside of bed frame and then safety pinned it to the mattress itself so it wouldn't get lost, all so I could use it to help tug myself upright. Due the fact that I'd get stuck a lot, unable to get myself up and usually needed his assistance on several occasions, he wound-up giving me the nickname "bug".

Therefore, as I mentioned earlier, I have learned that: borrowing, rearranging, redesigning and reassigning muscle and tissue (otherwise known as the extensive process of reconstructive surgery itself), *will definitely* cue the body to go into a tailspin. The muscles themselves do become slightly confused so therefore logically pain is sure to ensue. And just to recap: splicing, dicing, and relocating muscle does for sure cause some type of internal chaos and perplexity.

The end result, I live with pain daily…who doesn't though, right? It's always there, some level of pain and has become much like a devoted lover. It greets me as awake; kisses me goodnight as I fall asleep and sneaks up on me in the middle of the day. But the pain and I, see, we've learned to co-exist. I am not one for pill popping, so it has to be that way. Learn to live it, or let it consume you. And I won't allow it too; it will never ever control me.

Most days I simply ignore it, other days I use relaxation techniques to help ease the spasms and cramps which riddle my right side when they get bad; the pain and discomfort comes and it goes, flares and then ebbs with no particular rhyme or schedule. You just learn to live with it. And though sometimes it can be rather annoying, in all honesty I don't mind it so much, as it serves as a constant reminder that: Yes, I am alive!

It also occurred to me that all this pain and suffering might be a grand thing for the soul itself actually; as the quote suggests at the beginning of this chapter: *We must embrace pain and burn it as fuel for our journey…*

CHAPTER 15

If nothing ever changed, there'd be no butterflies.
                                    —*Author Unknown*

Odds and ends...interesting and/or humorous factoids...things you must know, but they don't tell you that I've learned along the way; in no particular order...

Chemo-brain is real! It also has long term effects. I know, I have it. It causes short term memory loss, inability to focus, and on occasion brain farts. While chemo brain is annoying, my cousin pointed out to me: So you have chemo brain. Big deal. If they would have told you you may suffer from it in the long run, would you have chosen not go through chemo? And what's worse? Going through chemo and being a survivor with the inability to recall things as quickly as you once did...or forgoing chemo and dying with your full memory intact? She had a valid point...therefore I don't mind chemo brain that much anymore.

When they propose to remove your breast, whether it's one or both, and they promise you "new ta-tas"....keep in mind they are not talking about breast enhancement. Nor will your new boobs look anything like the old ones. For some reason, this tid-bid escaped my logic. I seriously envisioned my new boobs looking like...well, that they would look like God-given breasts. They don't. They look like...well, I call them my *Barbie doll* boobs. Oh they're perky though. Firm and perky for certain. But something I must share, due to numerous people making comments such as *"Cool you got a free boob job."* or *"Wow, you get new boobs! You gonna flash everybody now?"* as if it was merely a breast enhancement job that I was planning. Um, no I won't be flashing them anytime soon. And, no, it's nothing even remotely close to breast enhancement. It's called reconstructive surgery for a reason. They recreate something from borrowed flesh, which somewhat resembles the shape of a boob. Plain and simple. There is nothing there to enhance, as they chopped the old ones off, therefore everything must be reconstructed, including the nipples *(and hope like hell those recreated nipples take, and don't scab over and fall off! Just mind-boggling to watch that happen.)* In addition, those recreated nipples have no "projection" whatsoever, so you can have those recreated nipples tattooed to give them color. It's an option. The running joke a friend of mine and I have, is tattoo mine HOT PINK or some other outrageous color. I haven't done so...yet.

In regards to the above....your new ta-tas will provide awesome cleavage. They will be awesome. You just have to accept them. Oh, and it is liberating to not have to wear a bra! Ever. Unless of course you want to.

Upshot of chemo...when you lose your hair, you lose all of your hair...so during the course of your treatments, you don't have to shave...anything. Just saying...

People sometimes do not know how to react when you

share the news of your diagnosis. Some people immediately breakdown and weep; others simply shake their head, and then (while I don't think they do so on purpose) walk around on eggshells and/or treat you like you are already dead. When friends looked at you—horrified after hearing the news of such diagnose and don't know what to say or do—hold your chin up and smile, then tell them: It's just a detour...I will survive this (I always added "and if I don't, I'll for sure go out in blazeof glory, kicking and screaming!"). Because along the journey of life, that is exactly what it is...a minor detour, and (along with great doctors and nurses and all of the various treatments you're sure to endure) it is the attitude you keep; that will help you get through this...

In regards to the above: Being a Stage III-B Advanced Breast Cancer Survivor, I am asked occasionally by new Warriors currently battling themselves, "How did you do it, how did you make it through, how did you survive?" and I never really honestly knew how to answer that question (other than to explain to them it's all in attitude and or a brief reply of "You just do it"), until I saw this saying...and thought it was prefect such a question that really has no right response. I am not sure who wrote it but it goes like this: *And once the storm is over, you won't remember how you made it through, how you managed to survive. You won't even be sure, in fact, if the storm is even over. But one thing is certain. When you come out of the storm, you won't be the same person who walked in.*

Epilogue

Suffering is good. It really sucks to go through it, but the rewards are unlimited and the greatest reward is the wisdom that suffering brings upon the victim. No one knows what he/she knows except others who have suffered the same. It brings about great changes in one's life and thinking. It brings one closer in understanding others and reveals ignorance and lack of experience. It brings greater personnel self-understanding and enlightens one to not only their strengths, but more importantly forces humility and knowledge of our ignorance of our self and others, and that what we know is nothing to what there is to know. Living is suffering. We suffer in all we do. You, my friend, have defeated a strong enemy. Your reward is a great treasure that you cannot keep. Unless it is given to others, it will rot and rust...so share it, you must.

—**Area51*Jedihunter*

The above excerpt came from an acquaintance of mine; a piece of advice which in part inspired me to actually share my journey with others. When I read that response, after a lengthy back and forth correspondence (debating and exploring life, death, cancer, and the trials of survivorship itself), I knew I had to indeed share my treasure; my journal of experiences which I'd kept along the way. Because if I did not, as he suggested, it would indeed rot and rust.

So while my story ends here, it is not really over, as I've realized that my journey has just only begun. While I still some days struggle with survivorship...I now have a treasure chest of experience of which I can pull strength from, and an angel watching over me.

People sometimes call me "A walking miracle" and then ask me, "How does it feel to get a second chance?" but mainly they want to know one thinkg: "How has it changed you?"

And honesty sometimes I think they are expecting

some type of profound response...are waiting for some grand words of wisdom. I have neither. I only have my treasure of experience of which to share with them. So I usually reply, "I'm still me, just slightly new and improved."

So, yes, the entire ordeal has changed me; on numerous levels. I've learned a lot from my journey...but sometimes it is just too hard to put into words. I've learned and try to be a better person. I've learned to let others help me. I've learned not to sweat the small stuff. I've learned unconditional love. I'm not afraid to speak my mind. I've learned to stop and smell the roses; literally. I've learned to enjoy life for what it is, in the here and now. Oh, I still make goals and strive toward them, but I've gained patience, and I'm not in such a rush to get to the end result now. And I still make mistakes...but I've learned that it is okay not to be perfect as I am only human.

Thank you for letting me share my treasure with you. Whether you are currently faced with having to battle this disease (or any type of cancer) personally, or you know somebody or have a loved one battling cancer themselves...my advice is this: Attitude is everything. Humor helps. And never ever, ever, lose hope (and if you have to borrow it from a friend, do so). For those three items are indispensable and are mandatory to go into battle with...

About the Author

Residing along the beautiful Mississippi, in a small urban eastern Iowa town, Deena is currently working toward acquiring her RN-BSN and enjoys writing both fiction and nonfiction in her spare time.

Proof

Made in the USA
Charleston, SC
13 August 2012